About th

Krishna Dhan Das completed his Bachelor's in Mechanical Engineering in 2002 and worked in Hindustan Aeronautics Limited (HAL), Aircraft Manufacturing Division, for over five years. Thereafter, he devoted his time to research in Vedic scriptures.

He began as a full-time preacher of the International Society for Krishna Consciousness (ISKCON) in 2002.

He is the Founder & Director of Samruddhi School of Leadership, an encouraging training and guidance forum for teenagers, under the banner of ISKCON.

He has conducted several enlightening symposiums for corporate executives and students across industries and educational institutions.

Praise for the book

"Krishna Dhan Das has poured out his life's experiences in this book in the form of wise words that are organized extremely well with apt anecdotes and concepts arranged in an easy to remember format.... will act as a handy guide to any youngster who wants to embark on the path to self-growth."

– Shubha Vilas
Author, Motivational Speaker, Leadership Professor

"Krishna Dhan Das has expertly woven immortal spiritual wisdom with practical solutions to contemporary challenges, making the book a compelling read."

– Gauranga Das
Author, Director - Govardhan Ecovillage

"A must-read book for personal as well as professional success seekers. It will help you create the life you deserve."

– Hrishikesh Mafatlal
Chairman, Arvind Mafatlal Group

"Krishna Dhan Das pulls together his decades of personal experience in mentoring people, inspiring success stories from various fields and a lot of research, and distills it all into a set of practical strategies to make you more motivated and more consistent at what you do."

– Dr Ajay Sankhe
International President for Global Foundation for Ethics and Spiritual Health (GFESH); Director, Bhaktivedanta Hospital, Mumbai

"Krishna Dhan Das has a penchant for making difficult subjects easy and relatable. This book is no exception. He has brilliantly combined personal stories with examples from the world around us, to teach us a concept that is so inherent to us – the desire to improve and contribute. I strongly recommend this book to men and women from all walks of life, and especially to those who often get overwhelmed or exasperated in the face of daily challenges."

– Vraj Vihari Das
Author and Mentor

"Simple, straightforward, and to the point... will change the way you approach your life. The principles laid down by the author will positively assist the reader realize their goals to turn their dreams into reality."

– Dr Rajeev Papneja
Chief Growth Officer & Technology Evangelist at ESDS Software Solution Pvt Ltd

"Simple yet effective practical tips on developing an improvement mindset that help you get into the zone where miracles can happen. If you want to excel and reach your highest potential with ease, this book is for you. It breaks this arduous process down into simple, doable steps and lays it bare in a structured way."

– Anand Pherwani
Vice President at America Sterling, Inc., Bloomfield Hills, MI, USA

"...an engaging life guide that shares many actionable tips. Use these tips and bring transformation in anything you want – whether it is health, career, relationships or life."

– Namita Purohit
Life coach, Founder - EASE Life Coaching Academy

"I sincerely find that this book will prove to be a landmark in transforming the life of every individual. He has explained in the most simple and easy to understand manner, about "Application of Kaizen in individual life" leading to Change for the better and leading towards success."

– Dr Om Prakash G. Kulkarni
Accomplished Scientist, Mentor, Adviser, Technology Provider, Certified Space Ambassador: National Space Society, USA

"Krishna Dhan Das, with his deep practical experience, unlocks the door to success by urging us to work on ourselves effectively, efficiently and enthusiastically."

- Manish Advani
TEDx Speaker, Founder & CEO MIMO Potentio, Award Winning Storyteller and a Business Leader.

LAUNCH YOUR LIFE TO THE NEXT LEVEL

It's time to find a new you

KRISHNA DHAN DAS

An imprint of
Srishti Publishers & Distributors

Srishti Publishers & Distributors
A unit of AJR Publishing LLP
212A, Peacock Lane
Shahpur Jat, New Delhi – 110 049
editorial@srishtipublishers.com

First Published by Bold,
an imprint of Srishti Publishers & Distributors in 2022

10 9 8 7 6 5 4 3 2 1

This is a work of non-fiction, based on the author's experiences and life-learnings. It provides practical solutions to everyday problems, but the recommendations given herein are in no way intended to be a substitute for professional advice and help.

The author asserts the moral right to be identified as the author of this work.

Printed and bound in India

To all my beloved mentors
who held my hand in
my improvement journey
and helped me grow in many fields.

To all readers
who want to take their life to the next level.

Contents

III

Acknowledgements

Walking through life, I have always seen myself as a student, surrounded by teachers who have enhanced the quality of my life immensely. I would like to express my heartfelt gratitude for all that I have been fortunate enough to learn from them.

To name all of them here would be impossible; however, three of the most prominent teachers in my life have been – H.D.G. A.C. Bhaktivedanta Swami Srila Prabhupada, the founder Acharya of the International Society for Krishna Consciousness (ISKCON); H.H. Radhanath Swami, the author of the international bestseller *The Journey Home-Autobiography of an American Swami*; and Shikshashtakam Das, who is life coach and mentor.

My special gratitude to Chaitanya Charan Das who acted as a prime mover and inspired me in my writing venture.

My special gratitude to all of my students and colleagues who helped me either directly or indirectly in this venture.

Special thanks to Pranav Mahajan for all the support in regards to writing.

And, of course, my warm thanks to the entire team of Srishti Publishers. Needless to say, my special thanks to Mr Suhail Mathur from The Book Bakers, who was not only my literary agent, but became an agent for taking this book to the next level.

Introduction

In my childhood days, I used to visit my grandparents' home every summer. I would yearn for this visit with my parents and younger brother. Usually all children tend to love their grandparents since they are very compassionate by nature and fulfill all the demands of their grandchildren. Our family, along with the families of my two uncles, would indeed be a huge gathering. I especially loved spending time with my grandmother, Ganga, who was very loving and caring. She would play with us and also narrate many fascinating stories.

One evening, she called out to us and gave us a pen and paper each. We were startled for a moment, since we identified anything to do with pen and paper as studies! It was vacation time and we were there for fun. Just the thought of studying was so off-putting.

She asked us to write our names on the paper and sit in a circle. We followed her instructions, after which she asked us to pass on the paper to the playmate on our right. We were supposed to write one good quality of the person whose name was written on the paper. We were to keep passing the paper in this way until it reached the person whose name was written on it.

That sounded interesting, so we started the task. No sooner did we realize that it was a very enlightening and enjoyable an exercise. It was self-congratulating to read about one's own good qualities and also self-elevating as we wrote about the things we appreciated in others. We heartily thanked our grandmother for such a lovely game and left for dinner.

Once done with the meal, while most of my family members left for a stroll, I stayed back to spend some more time with my grandmother. Another cousin stayed back since his favourite cartoon show was about to start.

I was chit-chatting with my grandmother when she said, "I saw all the papers you children submitted and observed that your handwriting is not so good. Why don't you try to improve it?" It was totally unexpected as my grandmother would always ask me about my friends, my school days, my hobbies, but never pointed out anything like this.

Taken aback slightly, I replied after some thought, "I write fast and maybe because of this reason, my handwriting is not so good."

"Oh! But why are you in such a hurry?" she asked.

"But the handwriting is readable, isn't it?" I smiled.

"Yes, it is readable, but not impressive" she nodded and added, "To score good grades, you should improve your handwriting."

"What do I need to do to improve it?" I questioned submissively.

"First of all, you need to accept that you need improvement. And then work hard towards it. Write more consciously. If required, reduce the speed of writing and take it slow. Practice writing one paragraph from the textbook daily and see the change over a period of time." She suggested lovingly and added, ["Every area of our life can be made better by conscientiously working on it. Never be satisfied with mediocrity. If you do, you will not find much fulfilment in your life. You will just be adding more days to your life rather than adding life to your days."] ✱

I expressed my gratitude to my grandmother for the eye-opening suggestions she has had showered upon me. I promised that I would follow her instructions and report my improvement to her.

As they say, in good times, the clock moves very fast. Subsequently, our time to head back to our respective homes arrived. Our schools were going to start soon and though we were not happy to leave, we had to. We touched the feet of our grandparents and took their blessings before we left.

After reaching home too, I kept my promise to my grandmother. I diligently practiced to improve my handwriting and the technique really worked. My handwriting improved noticeably. Though not that great, but it was certainly better than before.

My efforts were also appreciated by my grandmother as I wrote her letters regularly. After all, back in early 1990s, letters were the primary tools for communication.

"Never be satisfied with mediocrity." My grandmother's words kept ringing in my ears and I started improving myself in other areas as well – the method of studying, reading, speaking, playing and what not. The first-hand experience I had by improving my handwriting acted as a motivating factor. It was as if my grandmother had given me an 'improvement' pill to get rid of the disease of 'mediocrity'. I was really enjoying everything I would do and my school grades also began getting better.

Those few sentences from my grandmother during my summer vacation had really created a deep impact on my life and I was becoming a different person altogether. An improved person, to be precise. I stood second in the entire school in my tenth standard board exams, grabbed the third rank in college in the twelfth standard boards. I was also the top scorer for all the four years during my engineering education as well. And all the credit goes to my grandmother, and her advice. She changed the course of my life.

Just as the holy river Ganga purifies by removing the sins of those who faithfully take a dip in it, my life was purified of the contamination of 'mediocrity' after association with Ganga, my grandmother. Though she is no more as I write this book, I feel her presence in my life through her instructions.

'Always trying to improve and becoming a better person' attitude not only helped me get good grades during my academic stint, but also guided me in improving my relationships with others. It enhanced my professional life while I was working with Hindustan Aeronautics Ltd. (HAL). It also raised the standards in my spiritual life.

This attitude was all the more valuable when I became a monk in a monastery. Life of a monk is an offering for pleasure of the Supreme Lord and betterment of society. During my training as a monk, I was diving deep into scriptures. While systematically studying one of the scriptures, the magnum opus *Srimad Bhagavatam*, I came across an amazing character – Dhruva.

Five-year-old Dhruva preformed severe austerities of increasing order and pleased the Supreme Lord in just six months. Every month, Dhruva increased the severity of his austerities progressively. The word 'Dhruva' means 'one who is firm in his determination' And this little Dhruva did prove his name by his actions. I consider him as an 'Improvement Paragon' and could relate with his character very well. I came across many such figures who were constantly striving for improvement and learnt a lot from them.

As I progressed through my life as a monk, I was asked by the seniors to become a mentor and act as a guide to people after they got connected to the community. Accepting spiritual life requires some additions and some deletions. When I started playing my new role, I noted that while making these adjustments in life, many people struggled. Some of the youngsters who were habituated to getting up late in the morning struggled to wake up early in the morning, which is the best time for meditation. Some of the students, who were addicted to bad habits, had to engage in a scrimmage to give them up. In order to improve their conditions, I started helping people and offered them whatever I had learned in my life till then.

The task of a mentor is to offer a helping hand to a progressing aspirant. And so, the wisdom received from my grandmother was shared with multiple people, through me.

As far as changing habits and improving life was concerned, I started reading many books on such subjects and attended workshops. I also happened to meet and consult some senior monks. As they say, 'You need a guide, before you become a guide'.

Learning from ancient texts, modern books, experienced monks, experts in improvement and habit areas not only enriched my life, but also enabled me to support many other aspirants. Implementing this collective wisdom in my life was a fun and enlightening exercise. It was also an adventure to share the same with others.

'Share Your Care' was the slogan our senior mentor had instilled in us and I am writing this book in the same spirit of teaching and learning. I am a teacher at heart. As such, it is impossible for me to imagine not sharing what I have learned with others.

Your life is an amazing gift. How you choose to live, it is up to you. Your life does not always have to be in the spotlight or even on the mountain peak, but it can be continually moving forward.

I hope you find much value in these pages and will apply what you learn to whatever you do in your everyday life.

SECTION

I

1

Kaizen – An Ingenious Process

*"Excellence or Perfection is not a destination;
it is a continuous journey that never ends."*
                                    – Brian Tracy

It was almost the fag end of our one-year training program in Hindustan Aeronautics Limited (HAL), the company I worked with for a few years. Immediately after its successful completion, we were to be allotted some specific departments of work. Everyone was anxiously waiting for the allotment list to be displayed as they were eager to find out who got which department. Finally, I was allocated to the Industrial Engineering Department (IED). Some of my colleagues were given Overhaul department, some others were appointed for

Woodworks, someone for Scheduling, while some others were for Tooling complex, etc. Everyone was happy and excited at the prospect of working on the field and getting a chance to use all the skill acquired during the training. The training included learning about the organizational structure of HAL, soft skills, communication, team building, Russian language, Kaizen, technical knowledge of aircraft and things related to flights, among several other things. We all got immersed in training sessions as everything was new for us. One year passed by without us noticing much.

Sukhoi Su-30 aircraft was a buzzword in HAL as the company had recently got a deal to manufacture these aircrafts and supply them to the Indian Air Force. The company was gearing itself for production of the aircraft at a very rapid pace. New workplaces were being erected, new machines were getting installed, new departments were formed and several new people were employed (including a batch of fifty Executive Trainees (ET), including me).

All fifty ETs, armed with the fresh knowledge acquired during the training period, were now posted to different departments. We all had a great time during our training period and enjoyed each other's company. We were learning new things, making new friends and didn't feel any burden of responsibilities.

But after being posted to different departments, the scenario changed drastically. We all were immediately given new responsibilities. The target to be achieved and the deadlines to be met as the production of Sukhoi Su-30 was about to begin in full swing. Lunch hour was the only time where we ETs would meet in the canteen and share our experiences of our new departments and bosses. Everyone would eagerly wait for lunch time; it was the only time when we would get some respite from the heavy workload and share experiences with others.

HAL had the experience of the overhaul of MiG aircrafts, but Sukhoi Su-30 was totally a new venture. To cope up with new production requirements, many changes were being made in different sectors.

One day I received a notice from the chief manager, that in addition to my departmental activities, I also had to participate in Kaizen events that were taking place in various departments. HAL was now using TPS (Toyota Production System) tools to improve its working culture and Kaizen was a part of it. Though having got trained in implementing Kaizen theoretically during our training sessions, the actual implementation of it was totally new for me.

During the next one month, I was fortunate enough to participate in three Kaizen events, each lasting for five days. After the completion of these events, I could notice a dramatic change in the functioning of the department. A clean working environment, reduction in cycle time of a process, reduction of redundant activities, proper utilization of resources – these were just a few of the many noticeable changes. Though initially people were a little reluctant for any kind of change, but after witnessing the enhanced benefits and the improved productivity of the entire system, they readily embraced the change.

I was enjoying the task thoroughly, as I happened to get a hands-on experience of implementing the Kaizen. An added benefit was that the team involved many senior executives from other departments with whom I could directly interact with, hence learning a great deal. In one sense, Kaizen was just a modern word for the same methodology which my grandmother had taught me in my childhood – never be satisfied with mediocrity.

What is Kaizen?

Kaizen is a Japanese word, which was originally introduced to the West by Masaaki Imai in his book *Kaizen: The Key to Japan's Competitive Success* in 1986. Today, Kaizen is recognized worldwide as an important pillar of an organization's long-term competitive strategy.

When broken down etymologically, the meaning of Kaizen is:

'Kai' – Change and 'Zen' – Good.

Therefore, Kaizen means 'change for the better' or a 'continuous improvement process'. It's the same philosophy that helped Japan get back on its feet after the terrible destruction it faced during the Second World War.

Kaizen is a daily process, the purpose of which goes beyond simple productivity improvement. It is also a process that, when done correctly, humanizes the workplace, eliminates exceeding hard work, and teaches people how to perform experiments on their work using the scientific method. It also deals with how to learn to spot and eliminate waste in business processes. Briefly, the process suggests a humanized approach towards workers to bring about an increase in their productivity. In a layman's language, Kaizen brings continuous small improvements in the overall processes and eventually aims towards an organization's success.

Incorporating Kaizen into corporate thinking can deliver real competitive advantage. Many organizations all over the world have benefited from these techniques, including HAL, where having got to work and implement Kaizen, I witnessed a positive change.

At that time, HAL was gearing itself up with the help of the latest available technology and was working towards continuous improvement. When Dr A.P.J. Abdul Kalam visited HAL, he aptly mentioned, "Sky is the limit. This can be the motto of HAL."

Applying Kaizen in life

Is Kaizen relevant only for organizations and institutions? Obviously not!

Kaizen philosophy can be implemented in our daily lives as well. It's all about viewing our life as a work in progress, challenging ourselves to make continuous improvements and thus optimizing efficiency.

There is always a scope for doing things in a better way. Helmut Schmidt, a German politician, puts it aptly, "The biggest room in the world is the room for improvement."

An anecdote about Winston Lord and Henry Kissinger, two American diplomats, provides a glimpse into the idea of continuous improvement.

Winston Lord, during his time as special assistant to the then National Security Advisor Henry Kissinger, submitted a draft of a Presidential Foreign Policy Report to Kissinger for review. The next morning, Kissinger called Lord into his office and asked simply, "Is this the best you can do?"

Lord replied that he thought so, but he would give it another shot. So, he revised the report and resubmitted it.

The following morning, Kissinger called Lord into his office and asked him again, "Are you sure this is the best you can do?"

Disheartened, Lord again took the report and made improvements. The same scenario played out for six more times.

Finally, after Lord submitted the report for the ninth time, Kissinger again asked if it was the best he could do. This time, Lord replied, "I know this is the best I can do: I can't possibly improve one more word."

Kissinger looked up at him and said, "In that case, now I'll read it."

The moral of this story is that only your best work should advance to the next level, station, or person in the value stream. Does this happen in your life?

Perfection cannot be a specific standard; instead, it is an ideal which we should have as our goal. Continuous improvement is a theory that pursues the unattainable goal of perfection with the idea that there is always room for improvement.

Winston Lord devised various ways to improve his report eight times and although he eventually felt that he had exhausted every opportunity to improve his work, other opportunities to make it better probably existed. But since that report had to be produced and delivered in a certain time frame. Furthermore, Winston was having other responsibilities to take care of, he finally reached an improvement plateau after having reviewed the document eight times.

Herein lies another important aspect of continuous improvement. 'Best' and 'perfect' are two entirely different things. The best that one can do is the attainment of an unrivalled level of one's performance through one's own capabilities, through managing the circumstances and by getting a requisite experience in the work area. Perfection is a very open-ended concept. It is a never-ending progression where the sky is the limit.

I was fascinated by Kaizen, which resonated with the teachings I had received from my grandmother. I started applying it with all vigour in my corporate as well as personal life. No doubt, the results were amazing. During its application, I realised that Kaizen is not just a process, rather it is a mindset.

Key Takeaways

1. Change is constant. We should always be geared up for positive changes.

2. Kaizen can be used as a tool for overall development in all spheres of life.

3. Kaizen means 'change for the better' or a 'continuous improvement process'.

4. Kaizen is a daily ritual, the purpose of which goes beyond simple productivity improvement.

5. Kaizen brings continuous small improvements in the overall processes and eventually aims towards an organization's success.

6. You can list down areas that you think need your attention and work on them to achieve the desired results.

2

The Improvement Mindset

"Don't limit your challenges; challenge your limits. Each day we must strive for constant and never ending improvement."

– Tony Robbins
(American Author and Life Coach)

Human beings have a special advantage over animals in a sense that they can strive to do things in a more fulfilling manner – whether it be meeting the basic necessities of one's life, communication with others, or living a purposeful life. Animals never think of bringing some constructive change in their life, which is always a driving force for humans. New Year Resolutions are the resounding evidence of the same.

Humans have evolved from cavemen to spacemen due to this urge to always improve.

We all are aware of the law of gravity, aren't we? Anything that is thrown up, has to come down. The same law of gravity is applicable not just to things, but also to standards. We need to make efforts to go against gravity. For instance, we need a high power pump to take water from a lower level to a higher one. On the other hand, the reverse is quite natural.

Similarly, *our standards naturally gravitate downwards*. To uphold them, we need to apply continuous efforts. Therefore, to live a life of high standards, to always stick to our resolutions and remain fixed on our principles, one must put a great amount of unceasing efforts. Maybe we can learn this important principle from Kaizen and endeavour to apply it to our lives for continuous improvement in any area.

Lest you think it is a challenge only for you, let me tell you a fact. Upgrading to the next level is always a challenge. Improvement as a mindset needs to be developed; nobody is born with it.

'I can improve' and 'I need to improve' are the characteristics of this mindset. This is the mindset which actually carves out the difference between success and failure; between being a professional and an amateur. Dr Carol Dweck calls this the 'growth mindset'.

When Dr Carol Dweck and her colleagues became interested in student's attitudes about failure, they noticed that some student bounced back after facing all sorts of setbacks, while other students seemed devastated by even the smallest setbacks. After studying the peculiar idiosyncrasies of over thousands of students, Dr Dweck coined the terms 'fixed mindset' and 'growth mindset' to describe the underlying beliefs people have about learning and intelligence.

When students believe that they can get smarter, then automatically they understand that effort makes them stronger. Therefore when they put in extra time and effort, they achieve higher success.

On the contrary, fixed mindset is a tremendous liability. These students tend to think that their skills can't be further improved and hence deprive themselves of success.

How you perceive yourself is of paramount significance. Dweck's work shows the power of our most basic beliefs. Whether consciously or subconsciously, they strongly affect "what we want and whether we succeed in getting it." The understanding of our personality basically stems from our mindset. This can either propel us or prevent us from fulfilling our latent potential.

In the book *Mindset: Changing the way you think to fulfil your potential*, Dweck writes,

"...as you begin to understand the fixed and growth mindsets, you will see exactly how one thing leads to *another – how a belief that your qualities are carved in stone leads to a host of thoughts and actions, and how a belief that your qualities can be cultivated leads to a host of different thoughts and actions, taking you down an entirely different road."*

How this improvement mindset affects you?

A. Makes your life dynamic, pushing you out of your comfort zone:

A routine and comfortable life may tend to become mechanical and sometimes even boring. This boredom has become a deadly disease in today's society. Depression, escalating suicide rates, frustrating relationships and the need for a variety of amusements is a testimony to this. To substitute this boredom and to bring a change in the mechanical pattern of life, people try to introduce some things into their lives that might not be healthy. They could be depriving in myriad ways.

In contrast, constantly striving to improve our lives and trying to bring it to the next level creates dynamism. This can break the monotonous cycle and thus, boredom can be eliminated altogether.

An effort to build sustainable relationships, to upgrade our vocations and businesses, to read more wisdom books and to cultivate new good habits consistently pushes us out of our comfort zone. And once we are out of our comfort zone, life becomes more meaningful and fulfilling. This upward spiral of dynamism keeps growing and we become unstoppable in achieving higher growth.]

B. Creation of a positive pressure:

The right amount of pressure can even turn a lump of coal into a diamond. In terms of personal productivity, this pressure can be applied by one's own self or by others. Successful people continually put pressure on themselves to improve and perform in a better way. On the other hand, people who cannot motivate themselves have to be pressured by others.

To reach your full potential, you must develop this improvement mindset; a habit of putting pressure on yourself and not waiting for someone else to come along and do it for you. Here, the good news is that you feel better about yourself whenever you push yourself to do your best. The feeling of contentment that comes with it is unparalleled. Furthermore, it improves your self-esteem which acts as an antidote to depression. Gradually, you become self-motivated, as a result of which you don't need to depend on others for motivation to become the kind of person you wish to become. You don't have to wait for a car on a street where no cars pass.

When what we want to do is what we have to do, then motivation is self-generated. But when what we have to do is what others want us to do, then motivation is an injected steroid, which doesn't last long.]

C. Makes you view failures as stepping stones to success:

If you have the improvement mindset, you will not consider challenges in life as threatening. Rather, you will treat them as opportunities for burgeoning growth. You will look at a challenge as a step for further improvement.

When an average person meets with failure, then they define their identity as 'I am a failure'. On the other hand, when a person with an improvement mindset meets with a failure, they start thinking – 'How can I still improve?' and 'What can I learn from failure?' Only an improvement mindset can convert failure into a stepping stone for success, since for them, failure is not just a disappointment, but a new way of personal growth.

In 1978, a fifteen-year-old boy tried out for the varsity basketball team at high school. When the list was displayed, he couldn't find his name in it. Instead, he was asked to play on the junior varsity team, just because he did not meet the minimum height requirement. He was devastated and thought that it was the ultimate defeat. He locked himself in his room. Due to the agony of rejection which had pierced his heart, he cried a lot, venting out his emotional outpourings and mental distress.

After gathering himself up, he did what champions do. He let his failure drive him to be better and carried an improvement mindset with him. Playing in the junior varsity team, he pushed himself to the limit. From then on, getting trained relentlessly, he re-joined the junior team and eventually, his intense training paid off. His skill and expertise in the game reached a startling level that was way above everyone else's.

In the next couple of years, he grew five inches more and was able to make it to the high school team. The year after that, he made it into the All-American High School Team.

This boy is none other than Michael Jordan who is considered by many to be the greatest basketball player of all times. His relentless drive led him to break numerous records and become the most celebrated player in the history of the National Basketball Association (NBA).

Two Olympic gold medals, six NBA Championships and fourteen Most Valuable Player (MVP) awards were to his credit. That is how the basketball legend prove that through commitment and the spirit of improvement, one is capable of overcoming failure to reach truly incredible heights. He has been awarded the prestigious Presidential Medal of Freedom – the highest civilian award of the United States of America – for being an inspiration to millions of people around the world.

D. Enhances your creativity:

When you work with an attitude of improvement, various ideas about change and creativity follow. You would always want to improve yourself or the situation around you. History has witnessed many inventions born out of this attitude to improve constantly.

Fifteen-year-old Jack Andraka had a lot on his mind in the spring of 2011. A close family friend had recently died of pancreatic cancer. Reading up on the disease, the then high school freshman discovered that around 85% of pancreatic cancers are diagnosed too late, when patients have less than 2% chance of survival. The reason, Andraka learned, was that the best tools for early detection are both expensive and woefully inaccurate.

"I was like, there has to be a better way than this really crappy test," says Andraka, student at North County High School in Glen Burnie, Maryland. Jack, then a ninth grader, became interested in finding

a better early-detection diagnostic test. A typical teenager might have left it there, but Andraka, committed to improvement, dove deep into the scientific literature and approached many scientists at Johns Hopkins University.

Finally, under the mentorship of Dr Anirban Maitra, Professor of Pathology, Oncology and Chemical and Biomolecular Engineering at Johns Hopkins School of Medicine, he was able to develop a test. The diagnostic method he developed is more than 90% accurate in detecting the presence of pancreatic cancer's biomarker protein called mesothelin.

Andraka's work won him the grand prize at the 2012 Intel International Science and Engineering Fair in Pittsburgh, which comes with seventy-five thousand dollars in scholarship.

This improvement mindset made Jack Andraka, a fifteen-years-old boy, create a new diagnostic test for pancreatic cancer. His test is twenty-eight times faster, twenty-six thousand times less expensive and over one-hundred times more sensitive than the current diagnostic tests. Did you notice how a mindset drove him towards such a massive change!

By the way, the same mindset led to the invention of the electric light bulb by the mastermind, Thomas Edison.

E. You want to improve and not prove:

It was a day everyone was looking forward to! The day of declaration of results of the final exams. It was my third year in the engineering college, and all the students had high hopes from me as I had been the top rank holder in my first and second years. Our teacher was announcing our test scores and distributing mark sheets. I had scored 75.6%, which was better than last year's score. I was very happy, though the ranks were yet to be announced.

After distributing the mark sheets to all seventy students, the top three candidates were announced. Interestingly, I was ranked second. But I was still happy, which was a surprise to many students.

"What happened this time?" My friend teased me.

I smiled at the question and replied, "Rank is immaterial. My score is better than previous year and I am happy with it." I was becoming a paragon of 'improvement mindset'.

When you work with a mindset to get better, you are comparing yourself with your previous version. You learn your lessons from the past and try to improve upon them. You want to do a little better than yesterday, that's all! Your goal is improvement, and not the achievement. You want to improve and not prove anything to others.

As Charlie Munger aptly puts it, "Go to bed smarter than when you woke up." This allows you to focus all your attention on the task at hand and be in the present. The improvement mindset asks you to beat your previous self for the sake of improvement and not for the sake of defeating someone. You only want to be better than before, that's all.

Three-time Olympic gold medallist and ten-times world record holder in swimming, Rowdy Gaines shares his experience in the same way. At every practice, he would try to beat himself. If the coach asked him to swim one hundred meters in one minute and fifteen seconds, he would do it. But the next day, he would try to swim one hundred meters in one minute and fourteen seconds. Competing with himself and trying to improve every day, made him achieve all the success.

F. Makes you a curious and constant learner:

It's no surprise that many of the most successful people share one thing in common – they are all constant learners. They dedicate a significant amount of time for absorbing new information. When you have an improvement mindset, then you are constantly looking for new information in the concerned field. You give up the approach 'I have got it all figured out', 'I know everything' and so on. Rather, this improvement mindset makes the kid in you alive.

Wondering why I said kid? Kids are always curious and they question everything. They never stop asking 'why' or 'what if' and keep exploring what are the other possibilities. Improvement mindset makes you deliberately learn new skills, taking on new challenges, meeting new people, solving new problems and engaging yourself in all sorts of productive activities. In a quest to develop and fine-tune yourself, you start reading more new books. This opens up new vistas and creates newer ways of thinking, thus keeping your mind fresh and productively involved. For a person with an improvement mindset, growth becomes natural.

American author and motivational speaker Zig Ziglar puts it in this way,

"I'm a constant learner. You need to be a constant student because things change and you have to change and grow. And I emphasize the word 'grow'."

You need to ask yourself three questions if you want improvement in whatever you do, or if you want to launch your life from one level to another higher level. Let us see what these questions are.

Key Takeaways

1. A growth and improvement mindset ensures we keep striving to get better.

2. The best marker to get better is to compare yourself with your previous version.

3. For a person with an improvement mindset, growth becomes natural.

4. An improvement mindset can help you in many ways:

    i. Makes your life dynamic, pushing you out of your comfort zone

    ii. Creation of a positive pressure.

    iii. Makes you view failures as stepping stones to success.

    iv. Enhances your creativity.

    v. You want to improve and not prove.

    vi. Makes you a curious and constant learner.

3

Three Golden Questions

"Sometimes one question can change the course of your entire life."
— Anonymous

It was an arduous train journey from Mumbai to Delhi. I was reading a book, which I usually do during long travels. After long hours of reading, I needed a break, so I closed the book and looked at what other passengers in the same compartment were doing.

"What's this? This is a cat. And what's this?" A mother was trying to teach her baby by showing objects and things. Next to me, was a man who was completely engrossed in solving a crossword puzzle. Everyone around was surprisingly questioning and answering. They were absolutely preoccupied with one thing or the other. I tried to relate my observations with some scientific findings.

Our brain wants some subject matter to think upon so that it can learn something new by using myriad brain faculties of reasoning, rational thinking, discrimination, recalling, memorizing, etc. In that sense, the mind has an inherent inclination to keep itself stimulated. A question has the potential to stimulates our brain. Parents intuitively know about how to ask questions, answer them and then, again ask the same question and see if the child can recall. They clearly understand that questions stimulate one's brain.

If we wish to know how we can improve our lives, then the foremost thing is the necessity to ask pertinent questions to ourselves. Many a time, we end up asking the wrong type of questions, which result in utter dissatisfaction. These erroneous types of questions are something like this:

"Why don't I have enough in life?"

"Why am I such a loser?"

"Why are the successful people so lucky?"

"Why doesn't anybody appreciate me?" and many more.

While these questions have a power to engage the brain and spark intellectual energy, that energy is used to discern one's weaknesses and further emphasize upon it. This marginalizes the talents and resources we have at our disposal.

Instead of brooding over the aforesaid questions, the game changes if we ask a set of different questions to ourselves.

This can be done in a contemplative mood or while engaging in any kind of activity – whether it be writing, meditating, studying, cooking or anything at all.

With this, we can not only save ourselves from negativity engulfing us, but also tread on the path of progress more rapidly. Trying to answer the three golden questions can certainly change the course of one's life and lead it in a more productive manner.

The Three Golden Questions

The three golden questions which every contemplative person should ask oneself to progress meaningfully in one's life are:

1. What am I doing?
2. How am I doing?
3. Why am I doing?

1. What am I doing?

Advaita was my student, studying in tenth standard. He once approached me for a difficulty he was facing during his studies. Advaita was an intelligent student, but his problem was that he was not getting enough time for revising the chapters he had been taught, for solving the question papers and, for many such important things. He wanted to increase his focus so that he could get a good score, as tenth standard was a deciding factor for his career. Before meeting him, I had already contacted his mother to know about his schedule. His mother had also previously complained to me about his excessive cell phone usage, which led to squandering a lot of time.

I kept the meeting very light and crisp. I tried to offer some practical time management tips by applying an altogether different strategy.

'Stop using your cell phone altogether' type of answers would not have satisfied him. So, I told him that he could continue using his cell phone, but should make a note of his phone usage everyday and monitor the same for a week. He agreed for the seemingly simple solution and left.

Advaita met me after a week and showed me the report. He himself couldn't believe that he was using his phone for roughly two to two-and-a-half hours every day. He agreed that it was too much of time that was getting wasted. He wanted to work on it and change this habit.

I asked him, "What is that one thing you would like to do to keep the phone usage at a minimum?"

Advaita himself came up with the solution, "I will use my phone and social media only three times a day, fifteen minutes at a time. Maybe after breakfast, lunch and dinner."

I told him it sounded like a great idea and approved of the solution proposed by him. I asked him to keep track of the usage nonetheless. I also asked him to keep track of his study hours and meet me after ten more days.

Advaita was almost leaping when he came to meet me after ten days. He was very happy that the solution had worked for him. He had improved on his study hours by minimizing his phone usage. He had tracked not only his study hours and phone usage, but also his sleep timings, his time of eating, his television time and almost every single activity he would do in a day! He explained to me how he had also cut down on the mindless watching of television, which was taking a toll on his available time unknowingly. It was as if he got a magic wand to enhance his productivity and get more things done in the same available time.

Did you notice how I did not give him any kind of solution? He came up with the solution to the predicament he was facing, all by himself.

If you look at it in another way, I had only asked him to write an answer to the question, "What am I doing?" And this is precisely the reason why many habit specialists ask us to measure or keep track of our progress. They say, "The things we measure are the things we improve."

This measuring or tracking is nothing but answering the question, "What am I doing?" If someone is working on reducing weight, then asking this question will help that person to track everything which they pop into their mouth. This is what these steps-tracking devices do. They give you a number, a record, which you are tempted to break. It makes you become the best version of yourself.

If someone is working on saving money, then asking this question will help that person track every penny spent from his pocket.

This question aids us to bring our mind 'in the present' by making us more self-aware, keeping us focused on the task at hand.

The first step towards any change is self-awareness. What psychologists have discovered is that the very act of observing a behaviour tends to change that behaviour for the better. Answering this question, "What am I doing?" forces us to observe ourselves. When we observe ourselves engaging in any activity, we become more conscious of that activity, and we do it better.

For instance, when driving a car, it is a natural tendency of the car to go off track. Therefore, a steering wheel in the car helps it to keep on track. Similarly, this question acts as a steering wheel and bring our lives back on track. It does not let us get distracted and allows us to do what is most important for us.

I still remember that during my childhood, my mother would ask me and my younger brother, Gokul, to study in the hall and do our homework. In the meantime, she would be busy doing her other household chores. All of a sudden, while studying, Gokul would play some prank. He was the naughtier one, and his antics would land us fighting with each other. As soon as she got a hint that we had picked up a fight, our mother would just shout from the kitchen, "What's going on? What are you doing?"

Just having heard her voice, we would again get back to our studies, not giving her a chance to come to the hall and give us any further punishment.

Whenever I reminisce, I understand that just a simple question "What are you doing?" would goad us towards our main activity – studying. My mother used this question for us to not get involved in trivial activities and lose sight of important tasks at hand. Similarly, we can always ask ourselves this question 'What am I doing?' and steer the vehicle of our lives on the path leading towards our cherished goal, without getting distracted or tempted by trivialities.

'What am I doing? What am I observing or saying?' these type of questions can act as a powerful pause button before making any important decision. It can also save us from committing a mistake, eventually helping us to tread on the positive axis of improvement. Asking this question to ourselves may not necessarily add a high value to our activity, but it can surely help us to stop committing any seemingly minor errors for which we might have to repent later.

We are so accustomed to living with certain minor flaws or degrading habits that it's not always easy to identify them, let alone make corrections. But these unhealthy habits or behaviour patterns get tremendous momentum during the course of time and then, they act as a strong resistance against positive change. By training ourselves repeatedly to identify and solve the problems immediately at the stage of occurrence, we can avoid undergoing much more painful repentance in the future.

It's always better to ask ourselves "What I am doing?" rather than observing later, "What have I done!"

Do you know what is the basic foundation of the Toyota Production System (TPS) tools? It is Jidoka, a Japanese name for the same concept which we are discussing.

Jidoka was originally developed as a concept by Toyota's founder Sakichi Toyoda in the early 1900s when they were involved in textile looms. Jidoka provides operators the ability to detect an abnormal condition that could occur, and thus immediately halting the work. As the work immediately stops when a problem has first occurred, Jidoka highlights the causes of the problem and calls for immediate attention to the same. This leads to improvements in the processes that build in quality by eliminating the root causes of defects.

As they say, 'Nip it in the bud', asking the question "What am I doing?" is the tool for achieving this end.

A Continuous Check for Continuous Improvement

In its years of post-World War II rebuilding, Toyota fought to survive. That's when Taiichi Ohno, also called as father of Toyota Production System (TPS), instituted a new way of thinking and work culture. Ohno was never comfortable in his fancy office and preferred to be close to the action and in touch with reality. "Observe carefully to see the facts of a situation" was a mantra devised by him.

Ohno coached his budding TPS leaders to carefully observe the reality by drawing a chalk circle on the floor, telling them to stand in it for several hours observing reality, being open-minded and being undistracted by things which seemed more important for them to do. For others, this idea might have seemed absurd, but not to Ohno.

As a matter of fact, from Ohno's perspective, this practice of intensive observation imbued in them the habit of Kaizen thinking, which was necessary before they could coach others. He didn't ask people to confine themselves to the circle, but to dig through the clutter to see the essential problem. He was essentially making them ask the question "What am I observing?"

"Process visibility, seeing reality, is the primary way to see process problems and to identify kaizen opportunities" was what Ohno believed. To think of it in any scenario, you would agree that process visibility reveals problems to everyone, not only the managers. When something is amiss, workers can quickly determine the cause and take action. Process visibility also stimulates everyone to think of various ways to improve upon the process in general. Thus, empowered by the method, workers learn to self-manage processes and spontaneously improve them.

There are some areas in the organisation which can't afford even a single error. In my professional experience at HAL, I noticed that flight hanger and air traffic control were such areas. They were called the 'high-reliability areas'- meaning that their services are so vital and precise that they are all forced to find ways not to fail. Even if the warning is incredibly small, they had to immediately take strong and decisive action. Officers and crew are trained not to assume that the system will run perfectly. Instead, they look for the slightest signal that things are going askew. They are highly attentive because they are dealing with the lives of the fighter pilots, expensive fighter planes which amounts to crores of rupees and so on. Anyone who visited those sections in HAL could sense the pressure as the crew was constantly aware of this question – 'What am I doing?'

For those of us who aren't working under the pressure of life and death situations, it can be hard to see the little irritations in our day-to-day life. But still, we can train ourselves to implement this high-reliability strategy for ourselves, bringing this kind of meticulous attention to life's small warnings if we desire to take our life to the next level. We don't have to be paranoid about them, but we can't turn a blind eye to these little irritations, errors or negative habit formations.

2. How am I doing?

In 2004, nine hospitals in Michigan began implementing a new strategy in their Intensive Care Units (ICU). Almost overnight, healthcare professionals were stunned with its success.

Three months after it began, the procedure had cut the infection rate of ICU patients by 66%. Within eighteen months, this one method had saved seventy-five million dollars in healthcare expenses. Best of all, this single intervention saved the lives of more than 1,500 people in just a year-and-a-half. The strategy was immediately published in the weekly medical journal *New England Journal of Medicine*.

This medical miracle was simpler than you could ever imagine. It was a checklist. The checklist strategy implemented at Michigan hospitals was named the Keystone ICU Project. It was led by a physician named Peter Pronovost, professor at Johns Hopkins University, School of Medicine's Departments of Anesthesiology and Critical Care Medicine and Surgery, which was later popularized by writer Atul Gawande in his book, *The Checklist Manifesto*.

Pronovost started studying hospital-acquired infections in 2001, concluding that a simple five-item checklist protocol would greatly reduce infections when inserting a central venous catheter.

Checklist doctors should follow these steps:

1. Wash their hands with soap.
2. Clean the patient's skin with chlorhexidine antiseptic.
3. Put sterile drapes over the entire patient.
4. Wear a sterile mask, hat, gown and gloves.
5. Put a sterile dressing over the catheter site.

This five-step checklist appears to be a very simple solution used by Michigan hospitals to save many lives, but it was powerful. There were no technical innovations or cutting-edge procedures. The physicians were already aware of these steps, but they must have skipped a few of them unknowingly.

This was a clear case of physician Peter Pronovost's deliberating – 'How am I doing?' This thought, in regards to how the therapies, were being delivered helped in improving the patient's safety. And his strategy, though simple, brought a great revolution.

Many a times we tend to neglect simple things and might do an activity just for the sake of doing it. Answering this question 'How am I doing?' helps us bring out the best within us. It behooves us to think, 'Whether there could be another way of doing this?' It asks us not to do different things, but to do things differently. This question will incessantly ask for continuous improvement in any task or project which we may do, and ultimately, it will result in a masterpiece.

3. Why am I doing?

It was 1961 and President John F. Kennedy was visiting NASA headquarters for the first time. While touring the facility, he introduced himself to a janitor who was mopping the floor and asked him what he did at NASA. "I'm helping put a man on the moon!" said the janitor.

The President got the point. He understood the vision of the janitor and the part he played in it and thus, he could clearly make out that the janitor had a definite purpose.

'Why am I doing?', forces us to think about the goal for which we may be doing a particular activity. Answering this question directly hits at the core of our goal. When we have clarity of purpose, we will certainly put our whole-hearted efforts in whatever we do. All the successful leaders of the world started by answering this golden question. Leadership has got nothing to do with the post; it's about the purpose.

Answering this question can even lead us to do things which are seemingly 'next to impossible'.

Just bring a picture of a marathon runner in front of you – a woman or a man in running shoes, shorts or track pants, making her or his way through a crowd of cheering onlookers. How about a woman in her sixties? Running barefoot in a printed cotton saree hitched just a few inches above her ankles?

Lata Bhagavan Khare was a sixty-five-year-old resident of a small village located in the Buldhana district of Maharashtra. Her life was simple. She and her husband would go to a landowner's farm each day and make just enough to survive. Their house was small, but the food they got from the farm filled their stomachs.

The small amount of money they had saved throughout their lives was spent on getting their three daughters married. Now that they had fulfilled their responsibilities, they enjoyed the simple pleasures of life and each other's company.

One day after coming back from the farm, her husband told her that he did not feel so well. She tried all sorts of herbal medicines to help him, but he would not get better. The local government hospital diagnosed him with a serious infection, and they recommended that she should go to a bigger hospital that had better facilities. Lata was bewildered. They hardly had enough money for the fare to get a ride to the hospital, let alone the expensive tests prescribed by the doctors. With tears in her eyes, she told her husband the heartbreaking news. She felt overwhelmed with helplessness. How could she let her husband die in her arms?

Gathering up her courage, she then begged from the neighbours and relatives to put together the amount needed to go to a bigger hospital to save her husband's life. With the help she had received, they got to the big hospital in Baramati. The doctor moved her husband in the check-up zone. She discreetly sat outside the room with teary eyes, praying to god to save her husband's life.

The doctor came out of the check-up ward, and her eyes lit up, eagerly waiting to hear the well-being of her love. But fate had some other story written for them. Doctor said that these tests weren't enough to start the treatment; further tests and medications were required, which was going to cost them a hefty amount. Lata's vision was shrouded by the clouds of gloom. It seemed she had nowhere to go to get the money she desperately needed to treat her husband. She couldn't tolerate this helplessness.

She and her husband solemnly walked out of the hospital. Since they could not afford the commercial prices of the hospital canteen, they stopped by a samosa wallah at the bus stop and had two samosas on a piece of newspaper. As she ate her samosa and chutney holding the newspaper as its plate, she looked at the bold Marathi headline on the newspaper. The headline screamed about the Baramati marathon and its prize money. She winked repeatedly because of anxiety and all sorts of thoughts flooded her mind.

Next day, Baramati marathon was about to commence. Everyone geared up in their sports shoes, cozy shorts, track pants and sweat absorbing tees. And there she came! The sixty-five-year-old Lata, wearing a torn Maharashtrian-style saree, barefeet, tears in her eyes. She argued with the organizers because they weren't ready to let her participate in the marathon. She pleaded, begged and eventually, she made them approve her participation. She had never run a race in life, leave alone running in a marathon. She could not think of anything else, but the love she had for her husband. This race was a matter of life and death for her.

The marathon started, she hitched her saree just above her ankles. She ran like a wizard, like a sixteen-year-old teen. Nothing crossed her mind except that the only way to save her husband's life was to win the marathon and get the winning cash prize so that she could treat her husband of his illness. She didn't care about the hard-hitting rocks and pebbles on her way. Her feet began to bleed, her sari was soaked in sweat, but she kept running.

Lo and behold! She won the race. It meant the world to her. She was going to see her husband live. The crowds on the streets of Baramati clapped and celebrated her victory. People were flabbergasted on hearing the reason for her running the marathon and everyone saluted her. She was indeed a hero, but she didn't pay attention to all the applause. She collected the winning amount and made sure her husband received proper medication and treatment.

This is called devotion. She never thought about how she was going to win the marathon. She never gave thought to how she would run barefoot? How will she survive? She only ran with one motive in mind and that was to save her husband. She had the answer to the question 'Why am I running?'

In the same way, we need to have a good reason backing our efforts while performing any task. That way, we can make our lives meaningful by making a significant improvement. It's not only willpower that is essential for success, but also the *'why-power'* like that of Lata. All the 'hows' will be meaningless until our 'whys' are powerful enough.

So, start getting into the habit of frequently asking yourself these three golden questions and witness exceptional breakthrough in every aspect of life that is important to you. It can be relationships, health, finance, family, spirituality, business, education and so on.

There is a popular thought – 'Think before you act'. This 'think' must be nothing but taking a pause to answer these three golden questions.

Having established the questions to ask before setting out towards our goal, let us now have a look at the tools to ascend on the ladder of growth.

Key Takeaways

1. The first step towards any change is self-awareness.

2. Our brain cannot stay silent.

3. Our brain wants some subject matter to think upon or an object to which it can direct its attention.

4. It's not only the will power that is essential for success, but also the *why-power*.

5. A good way to keep the mind occupied is by questioning. A question stimulates our brain, wakes it up and makes it think.

6. There are three golden questions that can take you to success:

    i. What am I doing?
       By asking this question, we steer the vehicle of our lives on the path leading towards our cherished goal, without getting distracted by trivialities.

ii. How am I doing?
   This helps us bring out the best within us. It asks us to do things differently.

iii. Why am I doing?
   We hit the core of our purpose by asking ourselves this.

7. By training ourselves, we can identify and solve the problems immediately at the stage of occurrence.

8. It's always better to ask ourselves "What am I doing?" rather than observing later, "What have I done!"

9. All the 'hows' will be meaningless until our 'whys' are powerful enough.

4

Tools to Ascend on the Ladder of Growth

"Man is a tool-using animal. Without tools he is nothing, with tools he is all."

– Thomas Carlyle

After understanding how essential the principle of improvement mindset is in our daily lives, the obvious question which would arise is – how to improve?

When you want to commence any work, you need a tool for the same. If you are a writer, you would need a pen, paper, and other writing materials or maybe a laptop. If you want to go to a far-off place, then you need a vehicle. If your eyesight is not perfect, then you need to have a spectacle as an aid to regulate your vision.

On similar lines, the process of Kaizen also provides various tools as an aid. A tool called 5S is one of them.

The employment of the 5S concept into our program for implementing Kaizen fascinated me to a great extent. It tempted me further to delve into the nature of its great practicality and assured effectiveness.

5S, as we will see, is the foundation of all improvements. It is the key component of establishing a visual workplace. 5S was developed in Japan and was identified as one of the techniques which enabled 'just-in-time' manufacturing. It is a system used for organizing spaces so that work can be performed efficiently, effectively and securely. This system focuses on placing things at their rightfully designated places, keeping the workplaces clean, thus making it easier for people to do their jobs without wasting time or risking injury.

So, what exactly does 5S stand for?

There are five 5S phases. They can be translated from the Japanese as

1. Sort
2. Set in order
3. Shine
4. Standardize
5. Sustain

1. **Sort (*Seiri*)** – Seiri is the sorting out of all the necessary items from the unnecessary lot in a location.

2. **Set in order (*Seiton*)** – Seiton is placing all the necessary items at their optimal place for fulfilling their respective functions in the workplace.
3. **Shine (*Seiso*)** – Seiso is cleaning and inspecting the workplace, tools, and machinery on a regular basis.
4. **Standardize (*Seiketsu*)** – Seiketsu is to standardize the processes in the workplace.
5. **Sustain (*Shitsuke*)** – Shitsuke is to sustain the developed processes and never slip back into the anachronistic ways.

We can view our lives as a work in progress. We are often quite aware of and frequently scuffle with our various drawbacks, limitations, frailties of character, and imperfections in various aspects of life. We grapple with a teeming desire to liberate ourselves from these shortcomings, but what happens with most of us is that we become preoccupied with painting a utopian scene upon a dreamy canvas. Therefore, to improve upon our lives, we need to uninterruptedly monitor our unproductive and unhealthy behaviour patterns.

Many make new year resolutions, but do they last long?

Often, one is intimidated by the amount of change required to improve one's life. One feels short of time when it comes to commencing the processes of self-development. One feels it to be an arduous task to stick to good habits. This is primarily because we usually try to make changes with the help of wrong tools. And here it is where the 5S philosophy comes to our aid by offering us the right tools for improvement.

I am going to share with you 5.5 Ss – not the ones listed above and used in Kaizen, but the ones which can help you in making long-term positive changes in your life.

5.5 Ss of transformation:
1. Select your area of improvement
2. Start small
3. Schedule
4. Surroundings
5. Stay on
5.5 Seek help

Why did I call it 5.5, and not 6? I will tell you in a bit.

Let me share with you an interesting story which is a perfect example of the application of the above principles.

Milo of Croton was a sixth-century BC wrestler from the Magna Grecian city of Croton, who enjoyed a brilliant wrestling career and won many accolades in the most important athletic festivals of ancient Greece.

Growing up in Greece, Milo had always admired the Greco-wrestlers training in Croton. They were universally admired by the townspeople, possessed unbelievable strength and had bodies carved out of granite. Milo's admiration for such men was so strong that from a young age, he made the decision to become just like them.

In trying to achieve his dream, Milo 'discovered' progressive weight training.

The legend goes that one day Milo stumbled upon a new-born calf near his household. Rather than walk past the calf and continue his daily business, Milo hoisted the calf onto his shoulders and carried it upon his shoulders. The next day, Milo did the exact same thing and continued to perform the same task over a long period of time.

While most of the men would have become bored of such mundane activity, Milo nevertheless continued it with great persistence. As each day passed, the calf grew bigger, Milo started to bear more weight incrementally. After four years of the practice of carrying the calf upon his shoulders and walking back and forth, Milo could carry a heavy bull with ease. As the bull matured, Milo's body was constantly challenged and it had to adapt to bear the increased weight in order to accomplish the task. This contributed to Milo's increased muscular strength.

Milo went on to become a six-time wrestling champion at the Ancient Olympic Games in Greece and the most successful wrestler of his day.

This is how we can find the real-life application of the 5S principles of transformation:

Milo had always admired wrestlers, ever since his childhood, and thus wanted to become a successful wrestler himself. He selected his area of improvement (the first S, select your area of improvement). Milo did not try to lift a full-grown bull on day one. He began with a new-born calf. He started with bearing small weight (the second S, start small). He would do it every day; this means that he had a schedule for performing the task (the third S, schedule). Milo had carried on the practice at the same place. The calf, which Milo was carrying on his shoulders, was growing, maybe ounce by ounce every day and these tiny gains added up to significant weight in a relatively short amount of time. That is how he took advantage of his environment (the fourth S, surrounding). And lastly, he perseveringly practiced the task for four complete years, without fail. This shows his sustained effort (the fifth S, sustain).

These 5.5 Ss, similarly, have helped me immensely. I have shared it with many others who would come to me for counselling and guidance and it showed significant results there as well. These are time-tested tools. They can help you too, if you wish to take your life to the next level.

Read on to get a detailed understanding of the science of these 5.5 Ss.

Key Takeaways

1. It is best to see our lives as work in progress.

2. To improve upon our lives, we need to uninterruptedly monitor our unproductive and unhealthy behaviour patterns.

3. The 5.5 Ss of transformation that can change the course of your life:

   - Select your area of improvement
   - Start small
   - Schedule
   - Surroundings
   - Stay on
   - Seek help

4. Rather than being intimidated by the amount of change required to change our lives, we must focus on ways to start small and stay at it consistently.

SECTION

II

5

Select

"Things that matter most must never be at the mercy of things that matter least."
– Johann Wolfgang von Goethe

Being tired because of working throughout the day, I was anticipating to doze off to sleep. It was around 9:30 p.m. and no sooner had I just retired to my bed did the phone ring. I was reluctant to attend to that call, but wanted to see who was calling at that hour.

On the other side was Jyoti, a nice gentle lady, a teacher by profession. She considered me as her mentor so I took the call. She wanted to have a meeting with me in order to discuss a pressing issue. Though not urgent, but very important. We scheduled the meeting for the next day at 10 a.m.

Jyoti was ecstatic as she had given birth to a baby boy and which lady wouldn't be! I was just trying to recollect my last meeting with Jyoti and her husband Vinayak. It was the time when they were very excited about having a baby.

Next day, Jyoti came at the scheduled time. Her face was beaming with happiness as she approached me. We greeted each other and a discussion ensued. She was excited about playing a new role in her life. Happiness was gushing forth as she was sharing about her new motherly experience and attributes of her new-born baby. In a few minutes, I could notice the happiness fading away from her face. I sensed that there was 'something more important' she had come to share with me.

She started telling how there had been an apparent imbalance in her life after she had become a mother. She was a career-oriented woman and the year before becoming a mother, she had bagged the 'Best Teacher Award' in her institution. The following year, she took admission for the M.Ed. Course and was pursuing it concomitantly with her teaching profession and other household chores. Not only was she pursuing her M.Ed. course in her daily jam-packed schedule, she had also registered for some online teacher's training course to hone her skills.

She complained, "I am so frustrated! You know how much I love my baby, but he is literally taking all my time. I cannot do anything else."

She was upset because she felt that the baby was taking a toll on her career as all her extra activities were on hold and she would lag behind other teachers who were competing with her. Her constant anxiety was to achieve the 'Best Teacher Award' this year as well.

"Relax!" I consoled her. "And enjoy the nature of this new experience. You are not just a teacher, but also a mother now. To take care of a baby and nurturing him is the most important thing for you to do. No one can substitute for you. This is a one-time-experience in your whole life. Let everything else wait for the time being."

I told her to take a long leave from school and cherish this motherly experience. I gave her the example of Lokmanya Bal Gangadhar Tilak, one of the first strongest and foremost leaders who advocated the tenet of *swaraj* (self-rule).

When Bal Gangadhar Tilak felt that his body was delicate, he wondered how he could sacrifice his life for the country with a weak body! So he decided to improve his physique, at the cost of his studies during his first year at college. He took a break and started to exercise daily, regulated his food and engaged himself in sports. Gradually, he became an expert swimmer and wrestler. He developed his physique to such an extent that everyone marveled at his fitness.

Later, he continued his education, obtaining not only a bachelor's degree but also a law degree. At a later stage in his life, he started two weekly newspapers – Kesari and Maratha. He, being the front leader of the Indian

Independence movement, went on to become one of the greatest social contributors. He became so famous that he was not just an elected leader, but an accepted leader by the people. Which is why the title of 'Lokmanya' was conferred upon him.

I advised Jyoti, "Consult your mother and all other ladies regarding how to take care of the baby in a more nourishing manner. Read about parenting and do whatever you can to improve upon this area of your life. 'Best teacher' award is there in your arsenal, now it's time to add the 'Best mother' award."

By now, she had also realized that as the baby would grow and enter a different progressive phase in his life, she would be able to accomplish her individual goals and contribute in other areas in various ways. Since the baby was dependent on her for now, she was feeling this sense of missing out on other things.

Just as Jyoti encountered a dilemma in her life, we all are also caught in such confusions everyday. We just don't understand what we feel we should do, or what we want to do and what we should actually do. We get exasperated and grapple with the imbroglio when there is no link between the thing which we are doing and the thing which ought to be done. Therefore, identifying the most important things to do in life is of paramount importance. The same thing was realized by my friend Vicky in an amazing way.

Vicky was once commuting to another city by his car alone. He halted at one restaurant after driving for long hours. When he was about to leave the restaurant, he was unable to start the car. He tried over and over, for a long time, but to no avail. With all his tiring efforts, what he could do was to catch the attention of the restaurant owner. Seeing this, the helpful owner sent one of his servers to a nearby garage and got a mechanic for helping Vicky out.

After the mechanic came, he opened the bonnet and just kept observing the various wires and engine for about fifteen minutes. He then pulled out a hammer out of his case and hit at one particular part of the engine.

After that, he asked Vicky to start the ignition. The engine started. Vicky was mesmerized by this mechanic. He thanked him and asked how much he should pay him. The mechanic demanded a thousand rupees for having fixed the car.

Vicky was rather taken aback. "It's too much," he said. "You just hit at one part of the engine with your hammer. That's all! It shouldn't cost more than a hundred bucks!"

The mechanic replied candidly, "I have charged just one rupee for hitting the hammer and the rest of it for identifying where to hit it."

This incident illustrates the most important and basic principle of achieving success in one's life. Knowing which area to hit in our own lives is the most critical determinant of everything we can accomplish.

Just as the sun's rays, when focused through a magnifying glass, can create intense heat and fire, your intelligence and abilities, when concentrated on a key area, can enable you to accomplish more.

Tony Robbins remarks, "Controlled focus is like a laser beam that can cut through anything that seems to be stopping you. When we focus consistently on improvement in any area, we develop unique distinctions on how to make that area better."

When we talk about choosing an area for improvement, myriad things may come to our mind. We want to improve in each and every area of our life and we can see dozens of things that need improvement. But we need to choose that particular area which is most important, acting on which can make all the difference in our life. We just need to prioritize and use the strategy of elimination taught by Warren Buffett.

Warren Buffett, the self-made multibillionaire – who is consistently ranked among the wealthiest people in the world – reportedly gave his pilot a simple three-step process for prioritizing, which may come to our help when we want to prioritize the area of improvement.

Mike Flint was Buffett's personal airplane pilot for ten years. According to Flint, he was talking about his career priorities with Buffett when his boss asked the pilot to go through a three-step exercise.[1]

---

1. Refer to *https://jamesclear.com/buffett-focus* for more information on this.

STEP 1: You write down your top twenty-five career goals.

STEP 2: You do some soul-searching and circle the five highest-priority goals. Just five.

STEP 3: You take a good hard look at the twenty goals you didn't circle. These you avoid at all costs. They are what distract you; they eat into your time and energy, taking your attention away from the goals that matter more to you.

This technique can help you eliminate the inessentials of your life and find out the most important tasks to focus upon. You are not going to become Warren Buffett if you follow this method of prioritization. But you will surely get a better chance of moving closer to where you want to be in life.

Critical Path Method

What area should I choose for improvement can be well answered by the industrial term Critical Path Method (CPM).

CPM is one of the most widely used concepts in project management to handle projects which are complex in nature and involve significant activities.

In any given project, there can be hundreds of activities which are inter related. It can feel almost impossible to identify the most important activities; the ones if missed, will impact the whole project.

CPM was a project management technique created in the 1950s, and allows one to identify these important tasks and stay on track with complete focus on the essentials throughout the project. CPM not only maps the most important tasks in any given project, it also helps estimate the project completion date. How long a project takes often depends on the most important task that constitutes it. The path with the longest duration is called the critical path and it sets the overall duration of the project. By focusing on the tasks that make up the critical path, the project manager maximizes the chances of completing the project on time.

Certain resources (human beings, machinery and money) are generally common to different activities in a project. Critical path defines the activities to be given preference in the allocation of resources. Similarly, we also need to identify the critical areas in life which, when monitored and controlled carefully, can help us lead a meaningful life.

Italian economist Vilfredo Pareto (1848-1923) observed in 1906 that 20% of the people in Italy owned 80% of the country's wealth. Over a period of time, this observation became known as the Pareto Principle or the 80/20 Rule.

It is never exactly 80/20, of course! Sometimes it is 79/21 or 82/18, but the underlying principle is always true. It's not just a theory, but one of the greatest productivity truths ever discovered. This theory is applied all over the world by many multi-national companies as well as smaller firms.

Broadly speaking, 80% of all results come from 20% efforts. Richard Koch, in his book *The 80/20 Principle* remarks, "The 80/20 principle asserts that a minority of causes, inputs or effort usually lead to a majority of the results, outputs or rewards."

The point is, not everything matters equally; some things matter more than others. So, once we identify which 20% of activities in our lives are the most important, then we can be more effective by focusing our energy on them.

Therefore, first and foremost, we need to *select* an area where we want to focus our time, energy and resources for making some definite improvement.

A chain is as strong as its weakest link. Likewise, we need to identify which areas of our lives represent a weak link.

Exercise

1. Write down the most critical area in your life which needs improvement?

   _____

   _____

   _____

   _____

   _____

2. Where do you need to hit the hammer so that the car starts?

   _____

   _____

   _____

   _____

   _____

Key Takeaways

1. We need to prioritize and use the strategy of elimination taught by Warren Buffett.

2. Identifying the most important things to do in life is of paramount importance.

3. Eliminate the inessentials of your life and find out the most important tasks to focus upon.

4. We also need to identify the critical areas of life which, when monitored carefully, can help us lead a meaningful life.

5. Not everything matters equally; some things matter more than others.

6. First and foremost, we need to *select* an area where we want to focus our time, energy and resources for making some definite improvement.

6

Start Small

"The journey of a thousand miles begins with a single step."

- Lao Tzu

"Put your time to some constructive use," was the constant advice given by my father in my summer vacations during my school days. He worked in the Indian Army for about fifteen years and was very particular about one's health and physical fitness. He was especially worried about me, since my body was quite frail at that time. He would make me wake up early in the morning and urged me to go for a jog, to put some time into exercises.

Although I was already going for a run each morning since I was in fifth grade, he wanted me to do something more. After he voiced his further concern for me, I decided to join a gym where my friend Harshad would do his daily workout.

In my ongoing summer vacation prior to my entering the ninth standard, I visited a gym for the very first time in my life. Harshad told me to observe everything in the gym. I was very fascinated on seeing different kinds of equipment in the gym. Photos of great body builders, including Arnold Schwarzenegger, were stuck on various walls. Their physical fitness and looks were motivating me to do some workout. Harshad was busy in his workout and the instructor was busy in guiding the other members.

A series of benches were lined along the walls, on which people rested themselves and lifted different weights with both hands. One empty bench with weights kept on it caught my attention. Feeling tempted, I went forth to give it a try. I laid down and tried to lift the weight in a completely misinformed manner. Immediately having noticed what I was up to and sensing some impending calamity, the trainer present there literally yelled at me, "You fool! Do you want to break your back? The weight is about thirty kilograms and it's highly disproportionate for your workout, especially this being your very first day!"

Thereafter he gave me a very sound advice of starting the workout with very small weights under his guidance. A very crucial lesson dawned upon me – Start Small.

Those who have gone to a gym for body-building will say with conviction that they built their body by taking small steps, developing gradually. This principle holds true not only for physical body, building, but also in many other areas of life – like saving money for the future, building strong relationships, building a career, etc.

I remember, when I was child, I had received a piggy bank as a gift from my uncle. Many of you might have used a piggy bank in your childhood. It's a small container made of terracotta or metal, which kids use to save their money. After I received that gift, it was a pleasure to put single penny received into it. I continued this habit for a year and we cracked it open during Ganesha Chaturthi. I was amazed to see that I had saved around two thousand rupees, which was a big amount back in 1990s, especially for a child.

We installed lord Ganesha in our house, decorated the altar, donated notebooks and pens in an orphanage, purchased new books for my next academic year and obviously purchased a new piggy bank. I was amazed to witness a multitude of things we could do with the savings of just small amounts for a year. When we put the coin into the piggy bank, we don't see how much we have saved till now. It is as if the coin is in oblivion, in the unknown pit of darkness. But once opened, each and every penny counts and adds up to a massive amount.

Maybe the same thing happens when we take small steps towards self-improvement. We might feel that we are not doing anything substantial, that we are not bringing a groundbreaking change. But over a period of time, the change in our work area is quite huge, which one wouldn't have been able to do otherwise.

Unfortunately, today we live in a world where we are constantly bombarded to think of big things, about having big goals, skyrocketing dreams, bringing about sensational changes, thus sidelining the consistent small endeavours. Due to this attitude, we begin to feel that the incremental change wouldn't count much and that it wouldn't pay off ultimately. Though we celebrate milestones achieved, we tend to ignore the daily victories that were a stepping stones to ultimate success.

It is okay to keep a big goal in mind, to aim at the stars. But, it is also imperative to remember that we have to start from the ground to reach the stars. When we start small and work consistently, we can scale the biggest heights.

Every New Year's Eve, many of us make a list of life-changing resolutions. They may be about losing weight, getting more organized, reading more books, saving more, getting up early in the morning, writing more stuff and so on. We try to make these changes in their entirety, starting from the very first day of January. Yet over and over, we just can't summon up the willpower required for these sudden reformations, at least not for a long period of time. Many of these resolutions cannot stand the test of time, and mostly by the time we get ready to celebrate Makar Sankranti (which typically comes on 14th /15th Jan), they are out of our mind. At the maximum, they may last up to Valentine's day, mid-February, but that's about it.

According to the International Health, Racquet & Sports club Association (IHRSA), a trade group, 12% of new gym members join in January[2]. That would seem to suggest that some people are acting on their New Year's resolutions. But it doesn't necessarily mean they're sticking to them.

A 2009 study in the *International Journal of Sport and Exercise Psychology*[3] found that 50% of those who start an exercise program will drop out within the first six months.

Mark Twain, understanding the mind of resolvers, has said, "Giving up smoking is the easiest... I've done it thousands of times."

Many surveys suggest that a typical resolution is repeated ten years in a row. To end this annual ritual of failures, we need to change our perspective from the attempt to make some sensational changes in our life to the attempt of making small and doable changes.

Canadian adventurer Jamie Clarke, who reached the summit of Mount Everest twice puts it thus, "There's not only power in small, but magic, too."

We need to tap into this magic of small incremental steps to bring a sustainable change. And the same magic came to the

2. *https://www.usatoday.com/story/money/personalfinance/2013/01/16/gyms-new-years-resolution-rush/1779651/*

3. Wilson and Brookfield, 2009

aid of civil engineer Charles Ellet Jr., who was commissioned to construct a bridge over the Niagara Falls.[4]

Back in 1846, both Canada and United states, tired of waging war and wanting to capitalize on the magnificent falls they shared, agreed to unite the two countries by means of a bridge over the Niagara river. It was a great challenge because of the wide gap between the two cliffs and turbulent waters of the river. The site selected for building the bridge was along the Niagara Gorge, above the beginning of the Whirlpool Rapids.

After identifying the location, creating a line of communication between the two banks of the river was the project's greatest challenge.

The distance across the gorge at the chosen spot was around 800 feet and the drop to the river below was about 225 feet. The location was at the start of the Whirlpool Rapids, a particularly turbulent part of the Niagara river, just before the famous falls. Carrying the necessary cables over by water was far too dangerous due to the strong currents, so alternative and somewhat unusual methods had to be thought of to lay the bridge across. To Ellet's team, the task seemed next to impossible and they started

4. *https://blog.ferrovial.com/en/2016/02/the-story-of-the-first-bridge-over-niagara-falls-begins-with-a-kite/*
https://www.niagarafallsinfo.com/niagara-falls-history/niagara-falls-municipal-history/historic-bridges-in-niagara/the-first-suspension-bridge/

beings consider any change as frightening, especially when the change is too demanding or life-altering.

"This fear of change is rooted in the brain's psychology. It is a proven fact that when fear takes hold, it can prevent creativity, change and success," explains Dr Robert Maurer, a clinical psychologist on the faculty of the UCLA School of Medicine and the University of Washington School of Medicine. He is a founder of the Science of Excellence, and is a strong advocate of the power of Kaizen in personal as well as professional spheres.

"The mid-brain is where you will find a structure called the amygdala. The amygdala is absolutely crucial to our survival. It controls the fight-or-flight response, an alarm mechanism that we share with other mammals... The real problem with the amygdala and its fight-or-flight response today is that it sets off alarm bells whenever we want to make a departure from our usual, safe routines. The brain is designed so that any new challenge or opportunity or desire triggers some degree of fear. Whether the challenge is a new job or just meeting a new person, the amygdala alerts parts of the body to prepare for action. With that, our access to the cortex, the thinking part of the brain, is restricted, and sometimes shut down," explains Maurer in his book, *One Small Step Can Change Your Life: The Kaizen Way*.

Maurer believes that Kaizen can circumvent the brain's built-in resistance to new behaviour through small, conscientious steps.

One of my students Aswad was very inconsistent with his reading habits. On some days he would read a hundred pages of a book, and on some days, nothing. Sometimes even nothing for a week. As a result, he would read little, though he wished to read more and more books.

I thought of taking help of Kaizen, particularly the small step theory, to end his misery. I suggested Aswad to read only two pages in a day.

"Just two pages a day?" screamed Aswad in amazement, not knowing the power of taking small steps. He agreed to follow my advice and started reading two pages every day. He himself witnessed a drastic change in his reading habits after this. At some times, he would even read more, but that was bonus. He was able to stick to this habit of reading two pages even if he was ill, even if his schedule was too hectic.

I asked him about his realization after three months of practice. "Amazing and beautiful idea!" spoke Aswad, feeling grateful, "You don't need a strong sense of purpose to read just two pages a day. You simply have no choice but to do it daily. The target was so easy that you can't miss it. On some occasions, I read fifty pages, and even hundred on some days, but never less than two pages. Two pages was the bare minimum and I felt that was doable. I realized that my former goals were stress-inducing, but in this practice I felt liberated and totally stress-free."

Can you believe, someone's life changed by doing just one push-up a day?

Yes, Stephen Guise's life changed because of one push up a day. Stephen, before becoming an international bestselling author and blogger, struggled for long with lethargy regarding his exercise habits. For many years up until 2012, he faced disappointment and his life was a constant search and struggle for growth. After he got tired by repeatedly pursuing and failing to do the thirty-minute workout, he thought, "Whatever may be the case, I'll do at least one push-up."

He started to work on his resolve and did at least one push-up a day, which he calls 'The golden push-up', and changed his life for good.

"A mini productive habit though a very small positive behaviour forces you to do it every day; its too-small-to-fail nature makes it weightless, deceptively powerful, and a superior habit-building strategy," explains Stephen Guise in his book *Mini Habits: Smaller Habits, Bigger Results*.

Why Small Things Work

It is very easy to overestimate the importance of one sensational moment and underestimate the value of making small improvements on a daily basis. Most of us are convinced that for massive success, we need to make huge strides. One push-up in the case mentioned above was not even noticeable, but it was meaningful in the long run.

When we want to take small steps, 'stupid small' – the word coined by Stephen Guise – the friction is very less. Our minds generally resist any kind of change, specifically when the change is very demanding. When we want to add push-ups in our life, one push-up is almost friction less and doesn't demand much willpower. That is why it is easily doable.

When we want to read more books, or develop a steady reading habit, two pages a day is a small goal and rather easily manageable. When we want to write more, fifty words a day is frictionless. There is no pressure and no particular requirement of intense willpower to attain that. Due to this sustainable habit, we start becoming comfortable with these small steps. It might be tough to accept for some, but when we take these steps daily, we get a sense of achievement which goads us to do more, just as we saw with Aswad. Sometimes he would read more than two pages a day, the minimum he set out for himself, not because he had to, but likely because he started loving it.

Many people set a strict regime to follow and feel discouraged when they fail to achieve it. Life is unpredictable, and when you know you have an hour of exercise waiting to be done, the mind would protest. The mind likes to live in its comfort zone and take a path of least resistance. A strict regime throws the mind far outside of its comfort zone and it will definitely retaliate considering that as a harsh treatment from you.

Instead, by giving yourself a small target, you are comforting the mind, making it more curious to explore and expand the comfort zone. Soon, a half-hour exercise would be something that your mind is not only habituated to, but also addicted to. It will give you a sense of satisfaction, pleasure and accomplishment, and in turn will also keep you healthy.

When we achieve a small target, we don't just get a sense of accomplishment, but also an experience of doing the thing we were dreading. It breaks our fear and clears the way. That experience, in turn, acts as a motivating factor to do things consistently.

Law of Least Effort

Every ounce of our energy is precious and the brain is wired to conserve it in whatever way possible. It is human nature to follow the law of least effort, which states that when deciding between two similar options, people will naturally gravitate towards the option that requires the least amount of work. We are naturally motivated to do what is easy.

Every action requires a certain amount of energy. The more the energy is required, the less likely it is to occur. If your goal is to do a hundred push-ups per day, that takes a lot of energy! Not just physically, but mentally also, in motivating yourself for it.

In the beginning, when you are motivated, you can muster the strength to get started. But after a few days, such a massive effort feels exhausting. Meanwhile, sticking to the habit of doing one push-up every day, requires almost no energy to get started. And the lesser the energy the task requires, the more likely it is to occur.

Though you may be certainly capable of doing tough things, the problem is that on some days, you may feel like working hard, while on other days, you might just feel like resting. So, the lesser the friction you face, the more are the chances of keeping your commitment. The idea behind this discussion is not to make you do easy things, but to make it as easy as possible to do anything that pays off in the long run.

Exercise

Write down the small steps you can think of, upon which you may want to work on at least two fields of interest.

_____

_____

_____

_____

_____

_____

_____

_____

_____

_____

_____

_____

Key Takeaways

1. There's not only power in small, but magic as well.

2. When we take small steps towards self-improvement, we might feel that we are not doing anything substantial. And, we are not bringing a groundbreaking change.

3. Over a period of time, the change in our work area is quite huge, which one wouldn't have been able to do otherwise.

4. Daily small victories are stepping stones to ultimate success.

5. We need to tap into this magic of small incremental steps to bring a sustainable change.

6. There is no problem with thinking big. We need to 'thing big' but 'act small'.

7. By giving yourself a small target, you are comforting the mind, making it more curious to explore and expand the comfort zone.

just as
I have
from vari
full of pre
which I have
when som
a point to say
At this
of my year
ferry very

7

Schedule

"If you fail to plan, you are planning to fail."
– Benjamin Franklin

Just as everyone has some or the other hobbies in their lives, I have this leisure interest in memorizing Sanskrit verses from various archaic as well as contemporary texts which are full of profound meaning. Whenever I come across a verse which I find interesting, maybe while hearing a discourse or when someone sends me a thoughtful verse, I readily make it a point to memorize the same.

At the end of the year 2014, I decided to make a review of my yearly activities. I realized that in all I had memorized forty verses from different scriptures throughout the year.

Now I was about to enter 2015 and wanted to make some improvement in my habit of verse memorization. As a consequence, I decided to memorize a new verse every Monday and Thursday. And it was indeed encouraging that it was possible for me to memorize 104 verses a year.

I was amazed by this "scheduling" habit. I continued this habit of committing Sanskrit verses to my memory in a scheduled manner for every year to come ahead. By now I have memorized the entire *Bhagavad Gita* – an ancient Indian philosophical text, consisting of 700 verses and around 300 verses from *Srimad Bhagavatam* – another Indian philosophical text, along with other miscellaneous 200 verses from myriad other scriptures just with this habit of scheduling. Further, I made some improvisation in this habit of memorizing on the basis of the level of difficulty or complexity of the verses in getting committed to my memory. If the verses are simple, then I would schedule around 3-4 verses per week, whereas if I find them difficult, then just 2-3 verses in a week.

In the beginning, when I had started to memorize the verses, an element of spontaneity and abrupt motivation was involved. Later on, when I adopted the method of scheduling, I noticed that my productivity almost tripled. I was not only able to commit a greater number of verses to my mind, it also disciplined my approach towards work and increased the feeling of contentment. It encouraged me to progress further on these lines. Kudos to the process of scheduling!

Many a time people, according to their flights of fancy, set very high goals for themselves. And when they are unable to accomplish their respective goals, they are ready with numerous excuses like lack of motivation, determination, resources, etc. But in actuality, what they are actually lacking is right scheduling and proper planning.

Getting motivated to do something is really good, but the problem is, our motivation is based on our feelings. Those are unpredictable. Our feelings are dependent on many factors like weather, our physical and mental health, external stimuli, our energy levels, etc. Many of these things have a potential to alter our feelings. And for any change to be sustainable, we can't have a foundation which is so volatile. On the other hand, when we make a schedule, we don't have to depend on this volatile foundation of motivation. We just require our own strong willpower to stick to our schedule, whether we like it or not, and to do things exactly as they are scheduled.

In 2001, researchers[5] in Great Britain started working with 248 undergraduate students at a UK university in order to build better exercise habits. The aim was to minimize the rate of Coronary Heart Diseases (CHD) in people. Keeping

---

5. Sarah Milne, Sheina Orbell, and Paschal Sheeran, "Combining motivational and volitional interventions to promote exercise participation: protection motivation theory and implementation intentions," in *British Journal of Health Psychology*, Vol 7, May 2002: 163-184

the research period for two weeks, the subjects were divided into three groups.

The first group was the No-Intervention group, also called as the control group. They were simply asked to track how often they exercised.

The second group was the Motivational Intervention group. They were asked to track their exercise routine and to read some information on the benefits of exercise. They were encouraged to refer to any other material which provided them insights about the healthy habit of exercising. They were educated by circulating a factual health education leaflet containing information about the prevalence and nature of CHD and the effects of exercise on preventing the disease.

The third group was the Motivational and Volitional Intervention group. This group also received the same information as the second group to ensure equal level of motivation. However, they were also asked to formulate a plan about when and where they would exercise over the following week.

The subjects of the third group were asked to complete the following statements:

"During the next week, I will partake in at least 20 minutes of vigorous exercise on (Day or Days) _____ at _____ (time of day) at/or in (place) _____.

In the first and the second groups, 35-38% of people exercised at least once a week. On the other hand, 91% of the third group exercised at least once every week. It is more than double the normal rate!

Interestingly, the motivational interventions given to the second group seemed to have no meaningful impact on the behaviour.

The sentence filled by the subjects of third group is what the researchers refer to as 'Implementation Intention', which is a plan or a schedule you make beforehand about when and where to act.

The concept of implementation intentions was introduced in 1999 by psychologist Peter Gollwitzer. He coined two terms – 'goal intention' and 'implementation intention'.

Goal intention refers to what one intends to achieve and implementation intention refers to when, where and how one intends to achieve it.

According to Gollwitzer, holding a strong goal intention (I intend to reach 'X' level) does not guarantee goal accomplishment, because people may fail to deal effectively with self-regulatory problems during goal striving. The implementation intentions appear to be effective at enhancing the likelihood of goal achievement.

Implementation intention supports our goal intention by setting out in advance when/where and how I will achieve this goal. This strategy certainly helps people who are struggling with the problem of procrastination.

In other words, this form of advance planning or scheduling can bridge the intention- behaviour gap. Hundreds of studies are proof of the same that implementation intentions are very effective for sticking to our goals.

Once the implementation intention has been set, you don't have to be at the mercy of some sort of motivation or our fleeting memory to do things. You simply have to follow a pre-determined plan. A solid schedule fosters a well-worn groove for one's mental energies and helps stave off the tyranny of moods.

This implementation intention becomes the subset of what time management experts call 'time blocking'. Even though we might have set out important tasks to be done for a day, but we might also have experienced that the twin forces of internal whims of our mind and the external requests from other people or situations deviates us from following our schedule. Thus, we helplessly lose time and fail to stick to the schedule due to these distracting forces. It is at this critical moment that the concept of 'time blocking' comes to our aid.

Time blocking is the practice of planning out every moment of your day in advance and dedicating specific time blocks for certain tasks and responsibilities. Instead of keeping an open-ended to-do list of things you'll get to as and when you are able to, you must start each day with a concrete schedule that lays out what you will work on and when. When your calendar is filled with tasks you want to do, it's harder for others to steal your time and just as hard for your mind to say 'no'.

Time blocking acts as a guarding rail and prevents us from becoming a victim of what's known as Parkinson's Law – "Work expands so as to fill the time available for its completion."

By scheduling every minute of your day, you guard yourself against distractions and multiply your focus.

Obviously, it may happen that your estimate of time to carry out a particular thing may go wrong or some spontaneous important work may come your way, but you can certainly reschedule your plan since it is you who has created it.

The goal of scheduling is:
- Having a structured day.
- To get most important things done.
- Be aware of what I am doing with my available time.

Scheduling is really an invaluable tool. It helps to eliminate decision making; it helps us make the most of our limited self-command; it helps us fight procrastination; it helps us say no to temptations; it helps us identify time wasters in life. And most importantly, the strategy of scheduling helps us make time for the things that are most important to us.

Once we can tap the power of this advance scheduling technique, we can certainly unleash our true potential and hence, work on things that matter the most. As someone has rightly said, "If you don't make your schedule, someone will make it for you."

So, let us not give the control of our life in someone else's hand. Let us take full control of our lives by preparing a schedule.

Exercise

Make a DTP (Date, Time, and Place) format implementation intention for the small things you have decided to work upon.

Task	Date	Time	Place	Implementation goal

Key Takeaways

1. The strategy of scheduling helps us make time for the things that are most important to us.

2. Goal intention refers to what one intends to achieve.

3. Implementation intention refers to when, where and how one intends to achieve a goal.

4. Advance planning or scheduling can bridge the intention–behaviour gap.

5. Time blocking is the practice of planning out every moment of your day in advance and dedicating specific time blocks for certain tasks and responsibilities.

6. The goal of scheduling is:

   • Having a structured day.
   • To get most important things done.
   • Be aware of what I am doing with my available time.

8

Surroundings

"When a flower doesn't bloom, you fix the environment in which it grows, not the flower."

– Alexander Den Heijer

A. Surrounding Environment

Wrapped around the beautiful mountain ranges, picturesque landscapes, serene atmosphere, and situated amidst the pristine Tunga river is a place called Sringeri. It lies in Karnataka in the southern part of India.

I got the opportunity to visit this place with some of my friends. In order to spread the message of Sanatana dharma and guide religious and spiritual aspirants in the years to come, Adi Shankaracharya chose Sringeri for establishing his first *matha/ pitha* (monastery). Adi Shankaracharya was a great saint of the early eighth century, who propagated the doctrine of Advaita Vedanta philosophy and unified India, both culturally and religiously.

Once, I got the opportunity to visit Sringeri with some of my friends. While staying in Sringeri, far away from the city, equipped with less modern living, a question dwelled in my mind as to what made Shankaracharya choose this place, of all the places he had been to, for establishing his first monastery? This curiosity led me to a secret which was revealed by some of Sri Adi Shankaracharya's followers and also the spiritual mentors with whom I was travelling.

Tradition has it that Adi Shankaracharya was on the look-out for a convenient and holy place where he could establish an institution to spread the truths of Advaita Vedanta. When the Acharya came to Sringeri, he saw an unusual sight on the banks of the river Tunga. A cobra was seen spreading out its hood over a suffering frog, to give it shade from the scorching midday sun. Struck with the uncommon sight that a predator safeguards its prey, Sri Shankaracharya was convinced beyond doubt that Sringeri, the place of divine love, ensuring mutual co-existence of even natural adversaries. It was the right place to establish the very first of his four monasteries in India. After this, what Shankaracharya accomplished is witnessed by history – hundreds of books, thousands of disciples and cultural unification of India under one banner.

We can learn one noteworthy lesson from Shankaracharya – choose your environment wisely, which is favourable for your activity.

Environment is the invisible hand that shapes our human behaviour. We tend to believe that our habits are a product of our motivation, talent and efforts. Certainly, these qualities matter. But the surprising thing is, as time passes, your personal characteristics tend to get overpowered by your environment. Imagine trying to grow grapes in Himalayan mountains. You can be the most talented farmer in the world, but it won't make a difference. Snow is a very poor substitute for soil.

If you want to maximize your odds of success, then you need to operate in an environment that accelerates your results rather than hinder it. Even a small change in environment can give greater results. Just to give an example, a study from Brian Wansink (2012)[6] at Cornell University found that people eat 22% less food by switching from 12-inch dinner plates to 10-inch plates.

For instance, consider a drug addict who wishes to improve life by giving up drugs. Breaking free from the addiction is ultimately an inner resolution that they need to make and stick to. However, can they give up drugs if their house is next to a drug shop? It's almost impossible.

---

6. Plate Size and Color Suggestibility: The Delboeuf Illusion's Bias on Serving and Eating Behavior.
Koert Van Ittersum, Brian Wansink, *Journal of Consumer Research,* Volume 39, Issue 2, 1 August 2012, Pages 215–228.

The urge may attack them at any moment and if the facility to indulge is readily accessible, then even before their conscience gets activated, they will find themselves in the middle of a relapse. In such a case, though changing externals is not fully sufficient, but it is almost always necessary.

I run one institute for engineering students, with an aim to inculcate virtues by making them aware about our traditional Indian culture. I want them to know how practical it is and how, by following a Vedic lifestyle, would cater to one's holistic development in all spheres of life – not only just developing one's outer personality, which is the only focus in these modern times. The institute is known as the Bhaktivedanta Academy for Culture and Education (BACE). Here, all the students follow a regulated lifestyle, unlike the students in a hostel who think unrestricted freedom is the norm. All the students wake up early in the morning and report at 5:45 a.m. We have a short talk for half an hour based on Vedic scriptures, followed by yoga and meditation for some time. Thereafter, students take their breakfast and depart for their respective chores and colleges.

When they are back from college, they may take some rest and afterwards gather for evening prayers followed by dinner at 7 p.m. After self-study of about two hours, they go to bed at 10 p.m.

When all the engineering students have PL (Preparatory Leave), they happen to be full time in BACE. Keeping that in mind, the schedule is prepared in such a way that they are able to devote their maximum time for study every day, at least for about twelve hours.

One day when I went there as a part of my regular visit, I did not find one of my students there.

"Where is Sagar?" I curiously asked his room partner.

"Sagar has joined a library during PL," came the reply.

I was amazed. Here in BACE, students have all the facility to study. I wondered why Sagar had chosen to join the library.

When Sagar came back that evening, I asked him the reason for his joining the library. What he said was really eye-opening.

"As my PL started, I was able to study for only 6-7 hours. During the rest of the time, I was just chit-chatting and I became a victim of over-sleeping," he said. He also told me that 6 to 6.5 hours of sleep would suffice for him during regular college days, but nowadays, he found himself sleeping for about 9 to10 hours a day. He explained to me further that this was primarily happening with him because his bed and study table were close to each other.

Since one has to devote his whole time for studying in PL, Sagar used to take short naps and breaks in order to rejuvenate himself. But what eventually happened was completely the opposite. Either he used to sleep for long or he would spend a lot of his time in chit-chatting with others.

Now that he went to the library, he had to follow the rules of the library of not talking or to sleep or to keep munching something, etc. Everyone was so absorbed in their studies in a library that one cannot help but study. There was no luxury of lying down on a bed and relaxing. He said that he was able to study for about 12 to 14 hours a day.

With this incident, I came to the conclusion that it is indeed very important to have a conducive environment for accomplishment of our goals. Not surprisingly, Sagar scored 88% during his first semester, which was a great achievement. This certainly gave us the hint of restructuring BACE and have space for our own library for the students.

Designing our environment for improving our success rate is restricted not only to the field of studies, but for all the other fields like writing, playing, cooking, eating habits, etc. Suppose someone wants to develop healthy eating habits. In accordance to that, if that person places fruits and a bottle of water within his reach, then the chances of consuming those items are certainly more. Similarly, if a person wants to reduce the consumption of cookies and other junk food, and these items are kept near him, then it's very difficult for that person to overcome the habit of consuming junk or excess food. Our choices are not just based on what we are, but also where we are. And it is supported by the theory proposed by psychologist Kurt Lewin.

Kurt Lewin is considered by some as the father of modern social psychology due to his act of employing scientific methods and experimentation in the study of social behaviour. In 1936, he presented a simple mathematical equation known as Lewin's *Equation for Behaviour, which states, "behaviour is the function of the Person interacting within his Environment", or B = f (P,E).*

As our choices are affected by the environment, they can also be manipulated by the advertising industry to sell something by creating an environment. No sooner after Lewin's equation gained popularity, economist Hawkins Stern described a phenomenon called impulse buying – 'a shopper sees a product for the first time and visualizes a need for it.' On many occasions, customers tend to buy the product not because they want the product, but because of how the product is presented to them.

If you have noticed, items placed at eye level tend to be purchased more than those that are lying near the floor. And hence the saying goes, eye level is the buy level. For this reason, you will find expensive brands featured in easy-to-reach locations on store shelves because they drive the most profit, while the cheaper ones are at harder-to-reach locations.

We can see how a small change in what you see can lead to a big shift in what you do. Now you know how important it is to function in an environment that is filled with positive cues and not with negatives, if you really want to improve your life. The central idea is to create an environment where doing the right thing is easy and frictionless whereas doing the wrong thing is difficult and full of friction.

Life is a game and if you want to guarantee better results over a sustained period of time, the best approach is to play the game in an environment that favours you.

Choosing proper and conducive environment for all our activities including yoga, study, meditation, writing, cooking, playing can assure success in those activities. This is evident in *Bhagavad Gita*, where lord Krishna advises those who want to make progress in Ashtanga Yoga to choose a proper place for practice and also a proper seat.

> *śucau deśe pratiṣṭhāpya*
> *sthiram āsanam ātmanaḥ*
> *nāty-ucchritaṁ nāti-nīcaṁ*
> *cailājina-kuśottaram*

"To practice yoga, one should go to a secluded place and lay kusha grass on the ground and then cover it with a deerskin and a soft cloth. The seat should be neither too high nor too low and should be situated in a sacred place." *Bhagavad Gita*, 6.11

It is also evident from Vedic scriptures that not only devotees of god, but also the demoniac people were aware about the importance of choosing a proper environment for their success. Just to name few examples – Hiranyakashipu chose Mandar mountain to perform austerity and Ravana performed his austerity on Kailash mountain.

If demons can choose mountains and forests to perform better austerity in order to achieve their goals, just imagine how much we should be prioritizing and choosing our environment which is conducive for the accomplishment of our goal.

Be aware of the law of environment, which states that, growth thrives in conducive surroundings.

Remember, we need to be the designer and architect of our environment and not merely a customer of it.

Exercise

What possible measures can you think of to redesign your environment so that even a small improvement would be a very simple thing to do?

_____

_____

_____

_____

_____

_____

_____

_____

_____

_____

B. Surrounding People

> *"If you want to be a winner, hang around with winners."*
>
> – Christopher D. Furman

There were two extremely talented batsmen from Mumbai.[7] Their coach was Ramakant Achrekar. Each had a brother named Ajit. While one Ajit guided his younger brother in the right direction to give India a talented cricketer like Sachin Tendulkar, the other Ajit ruined his brother's potentially great career down along with him. This is the story of that unfortunate batsman whom Sachin used to address as "sir".

This person is Anil Gurav. He used to play for the Mumbai Under-19 team. Coach Ramakant Achrekar used to ask young Tendulkar and Kambli to watch Gurav's stroke play and learn from him. He was called the 'Viv Richards of Mumbai' and everyone thought he would be the first to go on to play for India. He says regarding his association with Sachin, "I was his captain at Sassanian (cricket club). He wanted to use my bat, but was too shy to ask me directly. The request came through Ramesh Parab (now international scorer at Wankhede Stadium), and I told Sachin he could use it, provided he made a big score. He said, 'I will, sir' and went on to score a century with my SG bat."

---

7. Ref- Interview of Anil Girav on AajTak- https://www.youtube.com/watch?v=c7syAtsQf10

However, he fell victim to some circumstances. His brother Ajit became a sharpshooter of an underworld gang. Police officers used to pick up Gurav and his mother repeatedly and severely beat them up to find out the whereabouts of his brother Ajit, sometimes detaining them for days.

By the time this ordeal ended, Gurav's cricketing career was also over. He took to heavy drinking. Everything was lost – his career, his dreams, all went up in smoke. He now lives in a shabby 200 sq ft room in Nalasopara in Mumbai.

Gurav says that he last met Sachin in the early 1990s at the Islam Gymkhana at Marine Lines, when he saw Sachin getting into his car surrounded by security guys. Sachin saw him and at once recognized him. He called him and spoke for a couple of minutes and asked him to come to his home.

While Sachin Tendulkar has become a legend of the cricket world who went on to achieve many highly-reverential awards, including Bharat Ratna and Padma Shri, Anil Gurav is an incorrigible drunk, striving to keep his family together.

Though both of them were highly talented, their talent was not the only component of success. This story illustrates how essential it is to be surrounded by people who will help you in accomplishing your goal.

Obviously, in the above story, Anil did not have a choice because his own brother acted as a hindrance to achieve his goal. But when we have a choice, we should be wise enough to surround ourselves with the right kind of people who will help us become what we truly want to be. And maybe that is why there's a famous saying, "Tell me who your friends are and I will tell you who you are!"

Association of great people around us can act as a catalyst when we think of improving our life and taking it to a higher pedestal. The kind of people we surround ourselves with can create a big influence on our behaviour, motives and results. The association you keep influences the way you think, speak, believe and do something to a great extent. American author, entrepreneur and motivational speaker, Jim Rohn puts this succinctly, "You are the average of the five people you spend the most time with."

Association of people with whom we hang around the most shapes us. According to research done by Harvard social psychologist Dr David McClelland, the people with whom you habitually associate with are called your reference group, and these people determine as much as 95% of your success or failure in life.

It is obvious, if you give it some thought. When we are with a set of people most of our waking time, we start thinking like they do, talking like they talk, reading what they read, watching what they watch, acting like they act and dressing up like they dress.

The people we interact with have a powerful influence over our lives.

I have seen how a new person taking admission in BACE is naturally surrounded by like-minded people who are seniors and are ready to help him. Usually, students take admission in BACE either in the first or the second year of their engineering.

But there are also few who walk in during their third or last year. I have practically witnessed the transformation in them as a person and even their marks making a progressive march compared to their previous records. Such is the importance and power of association.

Even our Vedic scriptures are replete with many examples and case studies of people who were transformed because of their association, whether intentionally or unintentionally. Ajamila, sage Valmiki, hunter Mrigari, Dhruva and Prahlad are just a few of the many examples who witnessed the transformation because of their association with some great personalities.

We are not going to walk our journey alone, and certainly not our improvement journey. We need to keep company of those who have walked longer, who are positive, who are ahead of us, who are willing to provide a helping hand rather than knocking us down and, who are themselves on an improvement journey. It follows that you can accelerate your personal growth in whatever direction you desire by spending time with people who are already placed where you want to go.

The central theme is to actively construct your social environment.

Don't let your association depend on chance, or how it has always been, but consciously plan for it. Just like a mango seed that is planted in fertile soil will grow into a mighty mango tree, the soil you choose to plant yourself in can take you to heights you have never imagined.

Exercise

Who are your friends?

_____

_____

_____

_____

With whom do you spend the most time?

_____

_____

_____

_____

What changes do you need to make in your social environment
if you want to make improvement in your selected work area?

_____

_____

_____

_____

_____

Key Takeaways

1. We need to be the designer and architect of our environment and not merely a customer of it.

2. Choose your environment wisely; pick what is favourable for your activity.

3. As time passes, your personal characteristics tend to get overpowered by your environment.

4. If you want to maximize your odds of success, then you need to operate in an environment that accelerates your results rather than hinder it.

5. Our choices are not just based on what we are, but also where we are.

6. A small change in what you see can lead to a big shift in what you do.

7. Life is a game and if you want to guarantee better results over a sustained period of time, the best approach is to play the game in an environment that favours you.

9

Stay On

"It does not matter how slowly you go as long as you do not stop."

—Confucius

Haven't we all grown up listening to the story of the hare and the tortoise? The tortoise, though not very skilled was nevertheless consistent and completely focused on its goal. The hare, on the other hand, got distracted from the goal and due to not being steady in its efforts, lost the race, in spite of it being more skilled as against the tortoise. The pertinent lesson which we learn from the story is 'Slow and steady wins the race.'

Steadiness and consistency in one's efforts are the key ingredients for success in any field. No one becomes a millionaire in a day. Neither does one becomes a successful athlete in one day, nor one becomes a film star in one day. The list goes on and on. Bringing you to the point – in order to reach the stage of perfection, we need to be persistent while pursuing the desired goal.

This is particularly true when we are about to use the 5.5 Ss tool. One of its components is – 'Start small'. When we begin by taking small steps towards our respective goal, we can't expect immediate and drastic results. In fact, in the initial phase, the results are almost invisible. There is not going to be any applause; no one is going to congratulate you for your efforts and discipline! Then what is the hope of getting the results?

The hope is the power of compound effect or exponential growth.

I came across a folktale by Demi- 'One grain of rice[8]'. It goes like this.

Long ago in India, there lived a king who believed he was wise and fair, as a king should be. The people in his province were rice farmers. The king decreed that everyone must give nearly all of their rice to him.

---

8. *http://jwilson.coe.uga.edu/EMT668/EMAT6680.F99/Martin/ instructional%20unit/day4.exponential/excel/grainofrice.html*

"I will store the rice safely," the king promised the people, "so that in time of famine, everyone will have rice to eat, and no one will go hungry." Each year, the king's rice collectors gathered nearly all of the people's rice and carried it away to the royal storehouses.

For many years, the rice grew well. The people gave nearly all of their rice to the king, and the storehouses were always full. But the people were left with only enough rice to get by. Then one year, the rice grew badly and there was famine. The people had no rice to give to the king, and they had no rice to eat. The king's ministers implored him, "Your highness, let us open the royal storehouses and give the rice to the people, as you promised."

"No!" cried the king. How do I know how long the famine will last? I must have the rice for myself. Promise or no promise, a king must not go hungry!"

Time went on, and the people grew more and more hungry. But the king would not give out the rice. One day, the king ordered a feast for himself and his court, even when there was a state of famine. A servant led an elephant from a royal storehouse to the palace, carrying two full baskets of rice. A village girl named Rani saw that a trickle of rice was falling from one of the baskets. Quickly she jumped up and walked along besides the elephant, catching the falling rice in her skirt. She was clever and she began to plan.

At the palace, a guard cried, "Halt, thief! Where are you going with that rice?"

"I am not a thief," Rani replied. "This rice fell from one of the baskets and I am returning it to the king."

When the king heard about Rani's good deed, he asked his ministers to bring her before him.

"I wish to reward you for returning what belongs to me," the king said to Rani. "Ask me for anything, and you shall have it."

"Your highness," said Rani, "I do not deserve any reward at all. But if you wish, you may give me one grain of rice."

"Only one grain of rice?" exclaimed the king. "Surely you will allow me to reward you more plentifully, as a king should."

"Very well," said Rani. "If it pleases your highness, you may reward me in this way. Today, you will give me a single grain of rice. Then, each day for thirty days, you will give me double the rice you gave me the day before. Thus, tomorrow you will give me two grains of rice, the next day four grains of rice, and so on for thirty days."

"This seems to be a modest reward," said the king. "But you shall have it."

And Rani was presented with a single grain of rice. The next day, Rani was presented with two grains of rice.

And the following day, Rani was presented with four grains of rice.

On the ninth day, Rani was presented with two hundred fifty-six grains of rice. She had received in all five hundred and eleven grains of rice, enough for only a small handful. "This girl is honest, but not very clever," thought the king. "She would have gained more rice by keeping what fell into her skirt!"

On the twelfth day, Rani received two thousand and forty-eight grains of rice, about four handfuls.

On the thirteenth day, she received four thousand and ninety-six grains of rice, enough to fill a bowl.

On the sixteenth day, Rani was presented with a bag containing thirty-two thousand, seven hundred and sixty-eight grains of rice. Altogether, she had enough rice for two bags.

"This doubling up adds to more rice than I had expected," thought the king. "But surely her reward won't amount to much more."

On the twentieth day, Rani was presented with sixteen more bags filled with rice.

On the twenty-first day, she received one million, forty-eight thousand, five hundred and seventy-six grains of rice, enough to fill a basket.

On the twenty-fourth day, Rani was presented with eight million, three hundred and eighty-eight thousand, six hundred and eight grains of rice– enough to fill eight baskets, which were carried to her by eight royal deer.

On the twenty-seventh day, thirty-two big bulls were needed to deliver sixty-four baskets of rice. The king was deeply troubled. "One grain of rice has grown very great indeed," he thought. "But I shall fulfill the reward to the end, as a king should."

On the twenty-ninth day, Rani was presented with the contents of two royal storehouses.

On the thirtieth and final day, two hundred and fifty-six elephants crossed the province, carrying the contents of *the last four royal storehouses – Five hundred and thirty-six million, eight hundred and seventy thousand, nine hundred and twelve grains of rice.*

Altogether, Rani had received more than one billion grains of rice. Finally, the king had no more rice to give. "And what will you do with this rice," asked the king with a sigh, "now that I have none?"

"I shall give it to all the hungry people," said Rani, "and I shall leave a basket of rice for you too, if you promise to take only as much rice as you need from now on."

"I promise," said the king. And for the rest of his life, the king lived fairly and nobly as an ideal king should.

This is the power of compound interest or exponential growth. When we talk about compound interest, it's the principle of reaping huge rewards from a series of small gains. Even though the results are massive in the end, during the course of action they don't feel significant. Therefore, all the mutual fund investment agencies ask their clients to hold on and stay for a long time without quitting in between, during ups and downs in the market. Patience is one of the important characteristics that needs to be developed if we really want to be in any field for long term.

Einstein said, "Compound interest is the eighth wonder of the world." And there is no wonder why and how seemingly insignificant small steps taken consistently over time will create radical difference. To reap the benefits of compound interest, you need to persevere and be there for a long term. If we quit in between, then the benefit is lost.

Life is not a sprint but a marathon where 'staying on' matters.

Getting started on the improvement journey is not very hard. Many people start their journey towards a goal and continue for some time, but eventually give it up before reaching their cherished goals. How often people start down upon a path and then give up on it entirely?

How many exercise equipment and weight sets are gathering dust at this moment across the country?

How many people start to learn a new language and give up soon?

How many books are lying idle just because someone had decided to read them, had started reading them, but then gave up just after few pages for some reason?

People often start something new out of excitement and good intentions but then give up permanently after encountering some kind of obstacle. Many of us, it seems, quit what we start far too early and far too often.

In fact, when people discontinue doing some things, they do so for a reason. Any of the following thoughts might come to you right before you quit what you are doing:

I am bored.

The effort is not worth it.

I can't do this, so I might as well give it up.

Many psychologists and trainers are working to find answers to the question – 'Why people give up?' While dealing with students and counseling them, I have noticed many factors which make people give up their journey towards their goals.

1. Lack of ownership

A third-year engineering student, Akash, from one of the reputed colleges in Nasik, came to me and informed me that he is no more interested in completing his bachelor's degree. It took some time for me to fathom what he was saying. I knew he was a hardworking student and would pass every semester with either higher second class or first class. I was surprised by his sudden change in attitude. I was taken aback and asked him the obvious question, "Why?"

He had already anticipated this question and it seemed to me that he was prepared to answer it. "I had a great fascination for yoga right from the tenth standard and wanted to make my career in the same field. But my parents forced me to pursue engineering after twelfth standard. I can, no longer, pursue engineering because of the stress and lack of interest. I cannot continue sacrificing my goals at the altar of my parents' whims," Akash breathed out.

This is not just the story of Akash, but many who want to do one thing but end up doing something else.

If we are doing something because someone else has asked us to do it, then it is called an "Outside-In" approach. It means that some force from outside is getting things done through us. This is where we think in a manner "I have to do" and therefore we fail to put our whole energy and concentrated effort to accomplish a particular task. The reason is that the motivational force is from outside. There is no ownership of the goal and hence, the tendency to become passive. Disinterest can peek at any moment, ending up in quitting one's journey. When goals lack ownership, it is very difficult to stay motivated and continue without a sense of purpose and meaning.

Hence, the continuation of journey is possible only when there is an "Inside-Out" approach, wherein the attitude is not that "I have to do" but instead "I *need* to do". That is how someone will have the motivation to do it without quitting.

2. Not willing to do the hard work

The path to reach our full potential and attain the desired goal is never easy. Our most cherished goals are also going to be the most challenging ones. When we find something more difficult than what we had expected, then it becomes a source of demotivation and eventually, we end up quitting.

3. Lack of patience

When we are obsessed with the result, we want it badly and want it now.

In today's fast-paced world, where everything is served instantly, we want the results of all endeavors also to be served to us in the same manner. But success is not obtained overnight. Unable to see any immediate achievement, people tend to give up.

4. Lack of discipline

Pursuing a goal necessitates a lot of discipline. Most people want to reach an end goal without having to sweat for it. Without discipline, you are lost and are destined to be servile to your mind, rather than having your mind to serve you.

5. Distractions

Achievement of any goal requires a great amount of focus. Any instant-gratification, which we succumb to, has a great power to distract us from the long-term goal.

Distraction is nothing but an alternative attraction for something else. When we get distracted, our goal does not receive the required amount of time, energy and resources from us. Slowly, with the passage of time, our commitment towards our goal fades away, along with our interest. The end result is that we end the journey towards the goal itself.

6. Seeing failures as permanent, and an end of all things

We can't anticipate the pursuit of our dream to be simple and effortless. Failures are going to be there. A vast majority of people see failure as a stumbling block and treat it as an adversity rather than converting it into an opportunity to learn a lesson and move forward. They view failure as permanent and give up on the journey, unable to tackle the failure.

Along with the six reasons listed above, there can be many more reasons because of which people don't continue pursuing their goals and ultimately settle for something less.

Consistency, steadiness and persistence are the key ingredients for success in any field.

"What makes people achieve great success and why?"

This question intrigued and obsessed Angela Duckworth, professor of psychology at the University of Pennsylvania. Her obsession led her to interview various leaders in business, art, athletics, journalism, academia, etc. She specifically conducted research on cadets of the United States Military Academy at West Point and students at National Spelling Bee. Through years of research, she concluded, anyone striving to succeed – whether it be parents, students, educators, athletes or business people – the secret of outstanding achievements is not talent and IQ, but the special and unique blend of passion and persistence which she termed as grit. After her thorough research, she wrote the book *Grit – The Power of Passion and Perseverance* substantiated by many case studies.

Various research studies have proven that talent and intelligence alone don't predict success. In fact, talent can hinder performance. On the other hand, effort is doubly important. In her book, she mentions two formulas–

1. You must put in effort to hone your natural talents into *tangible skills* through practice and improvement.

   Talent * Effort = Skill

2. You must also put in effort to apply those skills to solve real-world problems to attain *achievement*.

   Skill * Effort = Achievement

She writes, "Talent, how fast we improve the skill, absolutely matters. But effort factors into the calculation twice, not once. Effort builds skill. At the very same time, effort makes skill productive."

She has concluded that the sustained application of efforts towards a long-term goal is a biggest predictor of lifelong achievement. There are some limitations. Not all can make into NBA, but you can become the best player in your basketball team. Being gritty is hard, resisting endless temptations to quit or experiencing failure is extremely difficult to deal with.

"But we all have the ability to grow our grit," says Angela. "Together, the research reveals the psychological assets that mature paragons of grit have in common are four in number – Interest, practice, purpose & hope."

I have tried to summarize these four parameters in the following section –

1. Interest

Passion begins with something which you enjoy intrinsically. Research shows that people are enormously more satisfied with their jobs when they do something that fits their personal interests. Also, people perform better at work when they do what interests them. Angela tells her readers, "The directive to follow your passion is not a bad advice. But what may be even more useful is to understand how passions are fostered in the first place." Passion for the work is a little bit of discovery, followed by a lot of development, and then a lifetime of deepening. Interests thrive when there is a crew of encouraging supporters.

Newton had a fascination with questions concerning life and he always kept them alive at the back of his mind. It was Newton's deep interest and constant questioning that led him to a breakthrough that we call 'the Law of Gravity'.

What are the questions which intrigue you? Find those and you will find the capacity to stay gritty while trying to achieve something great.

2. Practice

Angela found in her studies that grittier people practiced more than their less gritty competitors. Grit is not just about the quantity of time devoted to interests, but also quality of time. Not just more time on the task, but also better time on it. Simply put, more experience will not lead one to excellence. What is required is deliberate practice with an attitude of continuous improvement. Olympic gold medal swimmer Rowdy Gaines, for example, said, "At every practice, I would try to beat myself. If my coach asked me to swim 100 metres in one minute fifteen seconds (1:15), then the next day I would try to swim 100 metres in one minute fourteen seconds (1:14)." One by one, these subtle refinements add up to dazzling mastery. In a personal interview Rowdy Gaines told Angela, "I swam around the world, for a race that lasted forty-nine seconds, to win an Olympic gold medal." This is what is meant by deliberate practice.

The refrain of all paragons of grit is "Whatever it takes, I want to improve."

3. Purpose

Interest is one source of passion. Purpose – the intention to contribute to the well-being of others – is another. The mature passions of gritty people depend on both. At its core, the idea of purpose is the idea that what we do matters to people other than ourselves.

Angela conducted a survey of sixteen thousand American adults to determine what the bigger contributor to grit is. The participants were asked to complete the grit scale. They were also asked to complete a long questionnaire concerning both pleasure and purpose. From their responses, she generated scores ranging from 1 to 5 for their different orientations to purpose and pleasure, respectively.

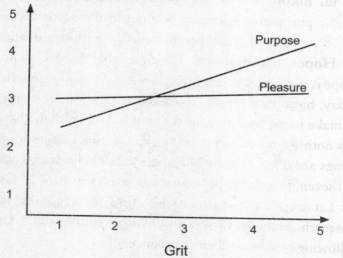

The data was plotted. It can be seen from the graph that grittier people are dramatically more motivated than others to seek a meaningful life. Higher score on purpose correlated with higher scores on the grit scale. Angela writes here, "Most gritty people see their ultimate aims as deeply connected to the world beyond themselves."

Angela finally gives three recommendations to cultivate a sense of purpose, all three borrowed from purpose researchers:

i. David Yeager recommends reflecting on how the work you are already doing can make a positive contribution to society.

ii. Amy Wrzesniewski recommends thinking about how, in small but meaningful ways, you can change your current work to enhance its connection to your core values.

iii. Bill Damon recommends finding inspiration in a purposeful role model.

4. Hope

Hope is not only expecting that tomorrow will be better than today, but also taking a responsibility and saying, "I resolve to make tomorrow better." The hope that gritty people have, has nothing to do with luck, but they keep going even when things are difficult. It resonates with an old Japanese saying, fall seven, rise eight.

Let us look at some interesting research revelations. Research has found that pessimists think in terms of the following phrases related to their fixed mindset:

I can't learn anymore.
I am what I am.
This is how I do things.

These people fail to move up on the ladder of success.

To be gritty, you need to awaken an optimist within you and start thinking in a different pattern (growth mindset):

I can improve.
I can do this,
My abilities are not fixed.

The same observation has been echoed by Carol Dweck as discussed earlier in the book, in the chapter titled "The Improvement Mindset".

Carol and Angela worked together to find the correlation between "mindset" and "grit", and concluded that students with growth mindset are significantly grittier than students with fixed mindset.

Angela puts it aptly;

"When you keep searching for ways to change your situation for the better, you stand a chance of finding them. When you stop searching, assuming they can't be found, you guarantee they won't."

Henry Ford is often quoted as saying, "Whether you think you can, or think you can't – you are right."

A fixed mindset about ability leads to pessimistic explanations of adversity and that, in turn, leads to giving up on challenges. In contrast, a growth mindset leads to optimistic ways of explaining the adversity and that leads to perseverance. You continue to seek your new challenges and thus, will ultimately make you grittier.

If we learn to take help from these researches and apply these four simple principles in our life, we can also become grittier and can 'stay on' in our journey towards our "selected" goal and become successful. Vince Lombardi says, "Winners never quit, and quitters never win."

To reap the maximum benefit of the compound effect, we also need to start early. The earlier we start making small changes, the more powerfully the compound effect works in our favour.

Once I was discussing the importance of starting early with one of my friends, Mayur. Though Mayur is a mechanical engineer by education, still having developed interest in finance, presently he works as a financial advisor to many individuals as well as corporations. He told me that this principle of starting early holds very true in the field of investments. He proved this point with an example which I am sharing here.

Suppose Mr Gupta began investing ₹5,000/- per month when he got his first job after completing his graduation from college at the age twenty-five. Mr Saxena, on the other hand, didn't save until he became forty. When both attain the age of 60, Mr Gupta will have more than 1 crore, growing at 15% interest compounded annually (assuming 15% rate of interest). While even if Mr Saxena starts investing ₹15,000/- per month (three times more than Mr Gupta's amount) from 40 years of age till he reaches 60, the normal retirement age, he will have less than 48 lakhs. Not just that, he would have invested 15 lakhs more than Mr Gupta.

(See the table attached to make the point clear.)

Mr. Gupta

AGE	Year	Year-end Balance	Interest (15%)	Cumulative
26	1	60000.00	9000.00	69000.00
27	2	129000.00	19350.00	148350.00
28	3	208350.00	31252.50	239602.50
29	4	299602.50	44940.38	344542.88
30	5	404542.88	60681.43	465224.31
31	6	525224.31	78783.65	604007.95
32	7	664007.95	99601.19	763609.15
33	8	823609.15	123541.37	947150.52
34	9	1007150.52	151072.58	1158223.09
35	10	1218223.09	182733.46	1400956.56
36	11	1460956.56	219143.48	1680100.04
37	12	1740100.04	261015.01	2001115.05
38	13	2061115.05	309167.26	2370282.31
39	14	2430282.31	364542.35	2794824.65
40	15	2854824.65	428223.70	3283048.35
41	16	3343048.35	501457.25	3844505.60

AGE	Year	Year-end Balance	Interest (15%)	Cumulative
42	17	3904505.60	585675.84	4490181.44
43	18	4550181.44	682527.22	5232708.66
44	19	5292708.66	793906.30	6086614.96
45	20	6146614.96	921992.24	7068607.20
46	21	7128607.20	1069291.08	8197898.28
47	22	8257898.28	1238684.74	9496583.02
48	23	9556583.02	1433487.45	10990070.48
49	24	11050070.48	1657510.57	12707581.05
50	25	12767581.05	1915137.16	14682718.21
51	26	14742718.21	2211407.73	16954125.94
52	27	17014125.94	2552118.89	19566244.83
53	28	19626244.83	2943936.72	22570181.55
54	29	22630181.55	3394527.23	26024708.78
55	30	26084708.78	3912706.32	29997415.10
56	31	30057415.10	4508612.27	34566027.37
57	32	34626027.37	5193904.10	39819931.47
58	33	39879931.47	5981989.72	45861921.19
59	34	45921921.19	6888288.18	52810209.37
60	35	52870209.37	7930531.41	60800740.77
AMT. INVESTED			2100000.00	
AMT. ACCUMULATED			10030531.41	

Mr Saxena

AGE	Year	Year-endBalance	Interest (15%)	Cumulative
26-39	1-15			
41	16	180000.00	27000.00	207000.00
42	17	267000.00	40050.00	307050.00
43	18	367050.00	55057.50	422107.50
44	19	482107.50	72316.13	554423.63
45	20	614423.63	92163.54	706587.17
46	21	766587.17	114988.08	881575.24
47	22	941575.24	141236.29	1082811.53
48	23	1142811.53	171421.73	1314233.26
49	24	1374233.26	206134.99	1580368.25
50	25	1640368.25	246055.24	1886423.49
51	26	1946423.49	291963.52	2238387.01
52	27	2298387.01	344758.05	2643145.06
53	28	2703145.06	405471.76	3108616.82
54	29	3168616.82	475292.52	3643909.34
55	30	3703909.34	555586.40	4259495.74
56	31	4319495.74	647924.36	4967420.11
57	32	5027420.11	754113.02	5781533.12
58	33	5841533.12	876229.97	6717763.09
59	34	6777763.09	1016664.46	7794427.55
60	35	7854427.55	1178164.13	9032591.69
AMT. INVESTED			3600000.00	
AMT. ACCUMULATED			4778164.13	

You see, Mr Saxena invested much more amount and still ended up with less than half of the money he could have had. That's what happens when we procrastinate and neglect necessary behaviours and disciplines. Don't wait for another day to start the small disciplines that will lead you in the direction of your goals.

Get started today and push on!

Exercise

Make a list of the tasks which you have left unfinished along with reasons.

_____

_____

_____

_____

_____

_____

What is core area of your interest? What are you doing to develop and deepen it?

_____

_____

_____

_____

_____

_____

Are you doing a deliberate practice?

_____

_____

_____

_____

_____

_____

_____

Identify what you need to do to 'stay on' your journey of improvement in your field of interest.

_____

_____

_____

_____

_____

_____

_____

Key Takeaways

1. In order to reach the stage of perfection, we need to be persistent while pursuing the desired goal.

2. Compound interest is the eighth wonder of the world.

3. There is no wonder why and how seemingly insignificant small steps taken consistently over time will create radical difference.

4. Life is not a sprint but a marathon, where 'staying on' matters.

5. The refrain of all paragons of grit is – "Whatever it takes, I want to improve."

6. To reap the maximum benefit of the compound effect, we also need to start early. The earlier we start making small changes, the more powerfully the compound effect works in our favour.

10

Seek Help

"One of the biggest defects in life is the inability to ask for help."

– Robert Kiyosaki

A. The Accountability Method

In our *ashram* (monastery), me and one of my friends, Sagar had undertook a task of memorizing the entire *Bhagavad Gita*. We both have the same hobby of memorizing verses. I would memorize one verse every day in the morning and he would also do the same thing. In the evening, we would sit together and test each other.

On one occasion, Sagar had to go home to attend to his sick mother and he was out of the ashram for almost a week.

During that time, I had no one to report to in the evening to test my learning. I still remember, during that week, my speed of memorization of verses reduced and I ended up memorizing a fewer number of verses compared to the previous week. After Sagar came back to the ashram, we resumed our daily evening schedule of testing each other and once again, we were on track. He also shared a similar experience – that when he was at home, he was not accountable to anyone. That he did not memorize any verses though he had enough time. We concluded that this 'accountability' towards each other is helping us directly or indirectly to move forward in our journey.

Accountability is a very powerful tool in our improvement journey. If we believe that someone is watching us, then we behave differently. When we believe that we may be held accountable for our actions – even when we're answerable only to ourselves – we show more self-command.

We all have observed that when the policeman is standing at road signals, with his baton and whistle, no one dares to break the traffic rules. And when he is not there, people tend to break the rules. (At least in some parts of India)

Even the sign 'This area is under CCTV surveillance' makes people watch over themselves and people are most likely to resist their temptations. And maybe because of this reason, there is a trend to install CCTV cameras in schools, banks, offices, near traffic signals, temples, parking areas etc. They also announce it loud and clear that you are under surveillance, to make people feel that they are accountable.

Once there were *pakoras* made in our ashram to celebrate Nikhil's birthday, one of the resident monks. Maruti was the one who liked pakoras the most, but he was resisting to take even one on that particular day, even though Nikhil himself was serving. Unable to resist myself over the uncommon scene, I asked Maruti for the reason. Unhappily, Maruti replied "I like the pakoras very much and I don't mind taking one, but tomorrow, I have an appointment with my ayurvedic doctor and he has asked me to not eat fried items during the course of treatment. The doctor is very apt in his *nadi* examination and can detect what you have consumed the previous day and would eventually scold me if the diet is not followed properly."

Some of us were aware about Maruti's indigestion problem and the treatment which he was taking. Those who were not aware were teasing him by relishing the pakoras with great delight. Though pakoras were Maruti's favourite, he was concerned more about the doctor and his examination the following day rather than his health, which was apparent from his reply. He could resist the temptation because he felt accountable to the doctor.

A chief benefit of fitness trainers, doctors, financial planners, life coaches, executive coaches, gym trainers, personal organizers and nutritionists, in addition to their expertise, is the accountability they provide. For many people, this kind of external accountability is absolutely essential in their improvement journey. Knowing that I am accountable to someone can be a powerful motivator.

On one occasion, Sachin, one of the monks in the ashram, was boldly announcing to all the monks during dinner – "I am not going to eat sweets for one month from tomorrow."

I knew he had no medical problem to make him do this, then why such a bold public statement? Later I asked him about his bold announcement to which he replied, "From tomorrow, the month of Kartik is starting and I have heard from our senior leader during his sermon that one should give up one's favourite thing for the pleasure of the lord during this month."

I nodded and said, "We are all aware of this starting of the Kartik month and also the austerities one needs to perform during this month. Everyone of us has taken some vows privately. But what is the reason of going so bold and making a public announcement?"

"See," Sachin started. "I am very weak in my commitments. Last year also I had taken one commitment privately, but could not continue for the entire month. Now I am announcing to all so that when we sit together for meals, I will be accountable towards everyone and even if I tend to break my commitment, there are so many others who will remind me of the same."

This is just another way to create accountability – to go public. In his memoir *The Writing of One Novel*, novelist Irving Wallace explained, "When you are a free and independent writer, without employer, without hours or deadlines, you have to play little games to force yourself into the actual writing. For me, one game is to announce ... that I have finally decided on my next book, that I am ready to write it ... to put my pride on the line."

When we don't follow our commitment made in public, we have a fear of being labelled as 'untrustworthy' or 'lazy'. We are not only failing to uphold our commitments to ourselves, but also fail to fulfil our promises to others. We want to be liked by others, trusted by others, loved by others and hence we care about their opinions. This is precisely, how we can take help of others by being 'accountable'.

While individuals can be accountability partners, it can also be useful to join an accountability group. Just as we see alcoholics... these people give and get accountability when they meet with like-minded people. And this has been seen as a powerful factor in giving up bad habits.

By being accountable to someone, either individually or to a group, is one form of taking help from others. But we can seek help of others in our improvement journey, especially in those areas where we lack awareness. Let's see how.

B. 'The Feed-forward Method'

His Holiness Bhakti Tirtha Swami, a very senior *sannyasi* (monk) and a disciple of His Divine Grace AC Bhaktivedanta Swami Prabhupada (Founder Acharya of International Society for Krishna Consciousness, ISKCON) had a very peculiar habit when he was a *brahmachari* and that really got me interested. He would go and meet his equals, seniors and ask them, "Is there anything in me that irritates you? What are things that I do improperly? Is there something I do that bothers you and how can I improve so that I can serve better?"

Basically, he was hitting that area of his personality which psychologists call a blind spot. You might wonder, what is this blind spot? Let me explain.

In 1955, American psychologists Joseph Luft and Harry Ingham invented a technique for improving self-awareness within an individual and they named it as Johari Window (The name is derived from the first names of the creators, Joseph and Harry). This window provides insights into the behaviour of yourself and others and can also be used for many purposes, including self-awareness, personal development, improving communications, group dynamics, etc.

The window as shown in the figure is divided into four quadrants that represents the four combinations.

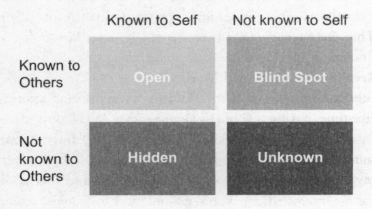

1. Open Space: Known to you – Known to others

This quadrant is about the behaviour that is known to you and also seen and acknowledged by others. Some of your talents, skills, abilities, weaknesses are known to you as well as to others.

2. Blind Spot: Unknown to yourself – Known to others

This quadrant is about the behaviour that is totally unknown to you, but acknowledged by others. It can cause others to talk about you because they can see something that you don't. Snoring during sleep, sweat odour, the frequent use of the same word while talking, fidgeting, etc., are just some of the examples of this.

This quadrant is of much concern to us. HH Bhakti Tirtha Swami, whom I was talking about, wanted to improve in this area by taking help of others.

3. Hidden Area: Known to yourself – Unknown to others

This quadrant is about the behaviour and skills that are known to you, but not acknowledged by others. People can keep certain information to themselves and not share it with others. For example, I am a flutist and might play flute in my free time, but I can keep it hidden from my colleagues.

The Hidden Area can also be unknown to a limited number of other people. I may share my hobby with some of my friends and then, they are also aware of it.

4. Unknown Area: Unknown to yourself – Unknown to others

This quadrant is about the certain traits about you, neither known to you, nor acknowledged by others. No communication exists in this Unknown Area. This quadrant is out of discussion because of the fact that both parties are unaware of it.

We all can take a good advantage of this wonderful concept of Johari Window, especially in the blind spot, where we are totally unaware of our traits but others are aware about them. We can certainly enquire from our friends, family members, colleagues and start the improvement journey.

Obviously, it requires humility to inquire from other people about your shortcomings. It is also challenging and requires a ton of courage to implement those suggestions in practice later. People tend to be defensive when someone offers them feedback.

In this case, because our focus is not on the past, but on the future (how to improve), and we ourselves have asked others about it, it's not called 'feedback'. It is called the 'feed-forward'.

Instead of rating and judging the performance of a person in the past, 'feed-forward' focuses on their development in the future. This concept of feed-forward was originally developed by a management expert Marshall Goldsmith who has a Ph.D. in organizational behaviour from UCLA and more than thirty years of experience in measuring and analysing behaviours in various organizations. According to him, successful people do not take feedback positively as they have a notion that they are already successful. When someone gives them feedback, they go in denial mode. Marshall's job is to help these CEOs by identifying a personal habit in them that is annoying their co-workers and to help them eliminate it. That enables them to retain their value to the organization.

Based on his experiences, Marshall has written a bestselling book *What got you here, won't get you there*. He writes, "My job is to make these successful people see that the skills and habits that have taken them this far might not be the right skills and habits to take them further." For helping these executives, Marshall first solicits "360-degree-feedback" from their colleagues and family members for a comprehensive assessment of their strengths and weaknesses. Then, he confronts these executives with what everybody really thinks about them. When they agree that they have room to improve, he shows them how to go about it.

It starts with apologizing to those who were affected by their flawed behaviour and secondly, advertising their efforts to get better. Marshall also teaches them the art of listening without prejudice to what their colleagues, family members and friends are saying and the miracle of 'feed-forward" methodology for eliciting advice from people on what they can do to get better in the future. This is what HH Bhakti Tirtha Swami was doing on his own (without Marshall coming to help him). He was taking the benefit of the 'feed-forward' methodology.

When we also develop courage and a little humility to ask others about our habits and behaviours that are annoying, or for some suggestions to improve in particular areas which we have selected to improve upon, then we are entering into the zone of blind spot. When we consciously try to make these changes, we start making improvements which seemed out of our reach before. This method works wonders. And that's because we can change the future, but not the past.

Sometimes the suggestions or 'feed-forwards' can even come from strangers! If you have the right attitude to look at those suggestions, then they can create wonders in your life. Here is an example of His Diving Grace A.C. Bhaktivedanta Swami Prabhupada.

Though Srila Prabhupada's spiritual master had departed from this world in 1937, his instructions constantly resounded in Shrila Prabhupada's heart, "You are an educated young man. Why don't you preach Lord's message throughout the whole world?"

This was what Prabhupada's spiritual master, Bhaktisiddhanta Sarasvati Thakura (BST), had asked Srila Prabhupada in the first meeting. Since then, after his spiritual master's departure from this world, Srila Prabhupada started many writing projects, including Back to Godhead magazine, which was initiated in 1944. He travelled to Jhansi and Delhi in his attempts to fulfil the will of his spiritual master and then finally settled in Vrindavan. He continued his writing and publishing work seamlessly. He would not only write, but also edit the material, purchase paper, print magazines and leaflets, distribute them to people and academicians who were interested.

Once a librarian advised Srila Prabhupada to write books because they were permanent. Newspapers, on the other hand, were read once and thrown away. He took the advice rather seriously, as if his spiritual master was speaking through this person. Thereafter, an Indian Army officer – who liked Back to Godhead *– suggested the same thing. As a dependent servant constantly meditating on the desires of his transcendental master and seeking his guidance, Srila Prabhupada felt his spiritual master's reciprocal blessings and personal presence. He felt a great inspiration to write books and thus he embarked on an English translation and commentary of Magnum opus* Srimad Bhagavatam.

Srila Prabhupada embarked on a journey to America at an advanced age of seventy, with his first three published volumes of Srimad Bhagavatam, *which he believed could change the hearts of the entire world. He established ISKCON in 1966 in New York and continued publishing books. What he achieved in eleven years till his departure from this world in 1977 is indeed astounding. The world has witnessed the magical feat – writing more than eighty books which would become the basis of the movement, establishing BBT (Bhaktivedanta Book Trust) for printing books, making thousands of disciples all over the world, opening hundreds of temples, farm communities and gurukuls (schools to teach ancient values and culture), just to name a few.*

Even after his departure, millions of his books are still being printed and distributed which are causing positive and elevating transformation in the hearts of millions of people.

This all began with the suggestion of a stranger to publish books. Obviously, Srila Prabhupada's firm faith in the instructions of his spiritual master and in the Lord made him successful in his endeavours, and that this stranger's suggestions were merely incidental. But nevertheless, this simple instruction by a stranger was a very powerful factor in shaping world history.

The question may arise in your mind, "Am I supposed to listen to suggestion from each and everyone around me, no matter what that suggestion is?"

The answer is no.

But you have to listen to those suggestions which take you closer to your goal. In case of Srila Prabhupada, the suggestion from the stranger to write books was in harmony with his spiritual master's instructions. His spiritual master has ordered him, "Whenever you get money, print books." And hence, when that stranger offered some suggestion, Srila Prabhupada could see that his spiritual master was speaking through this person.

In other words, the crisp message is – don't turn a blind eye to 'feed-forwards'.

Exercise

Are you accountable to anyone in your journey of improvement?

_____

_____

_____

_____

Muster some courage and with humility ask for feed-forwards from your colleagues about improvement in specific areas.

_____

_____

_____

_____

Key Takeaways

1. Accountability helps improve performance. If we know someone is watching and we are accountable, then we behave differently.

2. When we have an image to uphold in front of those who matter to us, we will be better equipped to stick to our commitments.

3. By working on the blind spots in your personality, taking the help of trustworthy companions, can be a rather enlightening exercise.

4. If you advertise your effort to get better, people around you will help you achieve the goal.

5. Filter suggestions and listen to those that take you closer to your goal.'

SECTION

III

Solutions to
Everyday Hurdles

During my talks based on the topics mentioned in the book, I received many questions from the audience. While engaging with their queries, I realised that many problems faced by people are similar in nature. I have tried to answer some of those questions which pertain to everyday problems so that my readers can benefit from them.

Q. I decide to get up early in the morning every night before I go to bed. But when the alarm rings, I don't know where my willpower goes away which was there at night. Any solution?

Ans. Yes, waking up early in the morning is very important but many people find it challenging. You are not alone as it's a universal problem. But that doesn't mean one can't become an early riser. I would like to offer the following suggestions which can be helpful:

1. First of all, you should have a solid reason to wake up early in the morning. If you don't have a sufficiently strong reason then, it will be very difficult to get up early. If your reason is compelling, then your why-power will also be firm! It will strengthen your confidence and determination to wake up in the morning.

   Imagine if you have a flight at 5 a.m. which you have to catch for an important work, then you will certainly have to get up at 2 or 3 a.m., so that you don't miss your flight. You basically start preparing your mind before going to bed to get up early. This mental preparation in the night, accompanied by a solid reason to wake up, is the key to becoming an early riser.

   As Dr. APJ Abdul Kalam has aptly said, "Dream is not what you see in sleep, dream is something which doesn't let you sleep."

2. Once you have a solid reason, you need to gather inspiration. I have observed that our inspiration to do a particular thing is directly proportional to our knowledge of the importance of that thing. I have seen many students eating bitter gourd after knowing about its health benefits even if they don't like it.

So, if you want to get up early, then start reading and watching informative videos about the importance of getting up early. If you know that many successful people from various fields get up early in the morning, then that can also inspire you to do the same. I am giving the names of few successful people from different fields who get up very early in the morning – Narendra Modi, Virat Kohli, Akshay Kumar, Amitabh Bachchan, Tim Cook, Vivek Bindra and list goes on and on...

3. You can't just rely on the inspiration to wake up early because ultimately, your body will demand its quota of rest. To get up early, you will need some preparations. One of them is to sleep early. You will agree with me that getting up early is a challenge, but an even greater challenge is to sleep early and especially when all entertainment devices are at your fingertips.

I personally set up an alarm not for waking up but for going to bed. And this is very essential. Once my alarm rings, indicating that the time to go to bed is approaching, I immediately shut down my laptop and switch off my cell phone. I read few pages from *Bhagavad Gita* and calm my mind to remove all anxieties. This ensures a complete and peaceful rest for me.

... situation, one of my friends, also struggled to get up early in the morning. While talking to him, I found out that he had a habit of scrolling through social media before going to bed. He also agreed that sometimes he got so hooked to watching videos or aimlessly scrolling over Facebook posts that he lost sense of time. I suggested him to stay away from all gadgets for at least half an hour before going to bed. He started following this regime and got immensely benefited from it.

You can also practice by setting up an alarm for going to bed and staying away from electronic gadgets for at least half an hour before going to bed. If you want to sleep at 10 p.m. then put an alarm at 9:30 p.m., and prepare your mind for sleep. Just disconnect yourself from the outside world during that half an hour and either start reading a book or listen to soothing slow music.

The second preparation that is needed to sleep on time is dark and regulated diet at night. If you like a very heavy meal before bedtime, then you will really find it difficult to get up early. So, eat light at night. Also the timing of your evening meal should be adjusted in such a way that there is at least two hours of gap between your meal and the time when you go to bed. This ensures

will be that you start getting up at 7:45 a.m. for 10-15 days. Getting up just fifteen minutes early will not be that difficult. It will give you a sense of accomplishment and also build your confidence. After 15 days, you can get up at 7:30 a.m. Gradually, you will be able to get up at 5 a.m. It will become your habit that will be long lasting.

7. You must have played cricket, right?

When you are batting, you need to be aware of the tricks used by the bowler if you want to succeed. In real life, our mind plays the role of a tricky bowler. And its tricks begin from early in the morning. Your alarm rings in the morning but your mind says, "Just sleep for five more minutes." If you either snooze or switch off the alarm and go to bed, listening to demands of the mind, then you are clean bowled. And when you wake up, you realize that five minutes has turned into half an hour, sometimes -even more.

Why should we allow our morning to start by getting clean bowled by the bowler called mind? Sleeping for five more minutes is not a problem but you develop the attitude of giving in. You tell yourself that what I decided last night is not as important as what the mind is saying so you listen to the mind.

It's not just about getting up early in the morning but it's about every aspect of our life. The impact of our morning habit is reflected in every area of our life. If you want to get up at 6 a.m. then, don't put the alarm at 5:30 a.m. and keep snoozing it. Put it at exactly 6 a.m. and get up as soon as it rings. As I usually say, 'You snooze, you lose.'

Q 2. **It is still very difficult to believe that small things can do wonders if done consistently. Could you prove it with an example?**

Ans. Yes, small things can certainly achieve wonders. They can help you attain great feats if you keep doing them consistently.

Let me share the story of an extraordinary person with you. At the age of 16, he encountered a large number of snakes that had died due to excessive heat after floods washed them onto the tree-less sandbar. It was during a major drought which occurred on Majuli reserve – the world's largest river island located in the Brahmaputra river in India.

Even at such a young age, he knew that someone had to do something. In 1979, he started planting a tree sapling in the barren soil, beginning with planting a bamboo and later, incorporating other species as well. At first, planting trees was time consuming until the trees started providing the

seeds themselves. As his forest grew dense so did the
number of inhabitants.

Soon, the forest was filled with hundreds of
species of birds. It also had deer, rhinoceros, tigers,
and even a herd of elephants, straying into
the forest three months out of the year.

His life began to change in the fall of 2007,
when a photojournalist stumbled upon him tending
his forest and wrote an article about him. He soon
gained the attention of the Indian government.
Gradually, the entire country got to know about his
wonderful work. He won multiple awards for his
incredible achievements and has started giving TED
talks. Ever since his story went viral in 2010, he has
travelled across the country and the world, to give
talks and attend conferences on climate change and
other environmental issues.

He is none other than Jadhav Payeng, also
known as Molai, the son of a buffalo trader, who
grew up as a poor farmer from a tribal community in
Assam.

Sixty-five-years-old Jadhav Payeng was conferred
the title of 'The Forest Man' by the Government of
India on World Earth Day in 2016, for turning a

References https://en.wikipedia.org/wiki/Jadav_Payeng
https://www.oneearth.org/reb_garden-jadav-payeng

...he transformed of 550 hectares (over 1300 acres) into a lush green forest, all by himself. It took close to thirty years for the land to turn into a forest.

To honour Payeng for his environmental activism and for planting one tree every day, the forest was named 'Molai' after him. He was felicitated at a public function arranged by the School of Environmental Sciences, Jawaharlal Nehru University on 22 April 2012 for his achievement. In 2015, he was honoured with Padma Shri, the fourth highest civilian award in India.

Jadhav Payeng would plant *one sampling a day* and continued the same for around thirty years. It is due to his consistent efforts that we see the spectacular result.

Payeng's story teaches us the power of small things and perseverance. Bruce Barton puts it aptly, "Sometimes when I consider what tremendous consequences come from little things..., I am tempted to think, there are no little things."

Q 3. I feel that I have too much on my plate and too little time at my disposal, what should I do?

Ans. You are not alone! Many people encounter such situations in their lives as well. Whether you are a software engineer, a housewife, a school going kid, manager of a company, an author or an entrepreneur – whoever you are, you must have faced a similar type of situation. Less time and too many things to do! Or you must have heard people complaining to you about such type of situations in their lives. Isn't it?

To solve this problem, start treating your life like a rose bush. Let me explain what does it means.

As a rose bush grows, it creates more buds than it can sustain. If you talk to an experienced gardener, he will tell you that rose bushes need to be pruned to bring out the best in both their appearance and their performance. Pruning is a horticultural and silvicultural practice involving the selective removal of certain parts of a plant such as branches or buds.

A rose bush isn't like a tree. If you never trim away some of the buds, then the bush will eventually exhaust itself and die. There are only so many resources to go around. And if you really want the rose bush to flourish, then it needs to be trimmed down not just once, but each year.

Your tasks at hand are like rose bushes; they need to be consistently pruned and trimmed down. And just like a rose bush, pruning away tasks, even if they have potential, allows the remaining tasks to fully blossom.

Just like the rose bush, we face constraints in our lives. We have a limited amount of energy to apply each day. It's natural for new projects to come into our life as it's natural for a rose bush to add new buds. But we have to prune things away before we exhaust ourselves.

In other words, it's normal for tasks and ideas to creep into your life, but full growth and blossoming requires pruning. It means ignoring all the things you could do and doing what you should do. Successful companies also follow this principle as they have one product or service for which they are known for, and that helps them to make the most amount of money. For example, Intel, Google, Apple have properly pruned their product range and are listed amongst most successful companies today.

To work on your most important goal and not get carried away by the whirlwind of ideas is also stressed in the insightful book *The Four Disciplines of Execution* by Chris McChesney, Sean Covey and Jim Huling. These authors have come up with these four disciplines, which guarantee execution, after working with three-hundred thousand leaders and team members across the globe.

The first discipline of execution is – focus on wildly important goal.

While explaining the first discipline, the book states, "Focus on the wildly important goal requires you to go against your basic wiring as a leader and focus on less so that your team can achieve more. When you implement this discipline, you start by selecting one (or, at the most, two) extremely important goals instead of trying to significantly improve all at once. We call this a wildly important goal (WIG) to make it clear to the team that this is the goal that matters the most. Failure to achieve it will make every other accomplishment seem secondary or possibly even inconsequential. This first discipline basically is the discipline of focus. The whirlwind robs from you the focus which is required to move forward.

And hence, sometimes we have to learn to say 'no' even to good ideas so that we can give a wholehearted 'yes' to the most important goal.

Q 4. Whenever I try to form a new habit, I am able to stick to it for some time. But, it is very difficult to maintain it for long. What can be done?

Ans. Yes, good habits are sometimes hard to start, but even harder to keep. Many habit experts suggest the use of 'habit tracker' which makes it easy to track how well you are sticking with your daily, weekly, or monthly habits.

When I had undertaken a project of learning all the 700 verses of *Bhagavad Gita* by memorising one verse daily, it was not an easy task. What I practised was that once I memorised a verse, I would just tick mark on that particular date on a calendar. Even though, I was just ticking on the calendar, I was actually using a 'habit tracker' unknowingly. Though

It was a simple tick mark, but it immensely benefited me.

Here is what I have learned from my experience. The huge goals of memorising all 200 verses was just mind-boggling/intimidating. So daunting that I was not even ready to start. But when I started with one verse a day and started ticking on the calendar, that tick mark was giving for a small win to look forward to the activity every day. I was able to physically see the progress that I was making and it was fuelling my motivation to keep going. Each small win was feeding my desire to continue.

When we get a signal that we are moving forward, we become more motivated to continue on the path.

I am tending the person who worked with to-do lists a lot of other time. Every time I made a tick mark on the calendar, it was a sort of gratification and my confidence boosted. I was experiencing a fresh good feeling, similar to what a money investor experiences when he watches his investment portfolio grow, or an author experiences when the length of the manuscript increased. And if it feels good, then I share more likely to endure.

It felt like a snowball effect as I kept memorising one verse a day. When I looked at all the tick marks in a row, I felt an urge to keep going. I was not fixated on the result. Rather,

I was just trying to keep the streak alive and become the type of person who doesn't miss even a single verse.

"Don't break the chain" has become my mantra. As I was gathering more momentum with each passing day, I started loving the activity of memorising the verses which was intimidating initially. Unknowingly, I was getting attached to the process and not the product. I was experiencing what psychologists call a 'flow state.'

If you want to take your life to a next level by starting and sustaining good habits, a simple habit tracker might be all you need. It will give you the necessary motivation you have been looking for.

There are many sophisticated apps available that you can explore or you can just use a tick-mark/cross-mark on calendar with pen, whatever suits you.

Q 5. **Is it at all possible to attain a stage where practicing a new habit is effortless?**

Ans. The good news is that yes, new habit can become effortless provided you give it enough time, energy and efforts to reach to that stage. Every new habit we try to cultivate follows a journey and it goes through four stages. Let me take you through the stages:

Stage 1 – Unconscious Incompetence

Stage 2 – Conscious Incompetence

Stage 3   –   Conscious Competence
Stage 4   –   Unconscious Competence

Sounds intriguing! Let me explain these stages through an example of child who is learning to ride a bicycle.

Stage 1:	At this stage, we are not aware of the fact that we don't know.
Unconscious	– The child doesn't know how to ride a bicycle.
Incompetence	– Nor can the child ride a bicycle.

Stage 2:	At this stage, we know that we don't know.
Conscious	– The child is aware of riding a bicycle.
Incompetence	– But he can't ride one.

Stage 3:	– At this stage, we are aware of the fact that we know.
Conscious	– To ride a bicycle, the child has to concentrate hard.
Competence	– With conscious thought and effort, the child is competent to ride a bicycle.

Stage 4:	– At this stage, we don't know that we know.
Unconscious	– The child has now practiced enough that he doesn't have to think about 'how to ride'.

Competence   – He can wave to others while riding, because the behaviour pattern has become automatic!

When we were children, learning a bicycle was initially intimidating, but as we practiced consistently with patience, we became perfect and reached the fourth stage. And the same holds true in acquiring a new skill, learning a new language or mastering a new game for that matter.

Similarly, by practicing any habit with patience and keeping your eyes not on the end result but on the process, your habit can become effortless.

Q 6.   **What is the exact meaning of living a balanced life and how to achieve that balance?**

Ans.   There are multiple dimensions to our life. Learning about these dimensions will enable us to understand the things which are worthy of our time and help us to live a balanced life. Just as a car balances on four wheels, we must balance the four crucial dimensions of our life – physical dimension, mental dimension, social dimension and spiritual dimension.

The Physical dimension:

It is mentioned in Upanishads, *shariramadyam khalu dharma sadhanam*, meaning our body is the first instrument or the tool for doing all our duties.

The instrument has to be cared for properly so that all functions, which an instrument is supposed to perform, can be executed effectively.

You must have seen how doctors, draftsmen and warriors take a good care of their tools. Similarly, physical dimension involves taking a good care of our body – eating the right kind of food, at the right time and in right quantity, sleeping at the right time and in right quantity, and exercising on a regular basis.

We can't turn a blind eye to our basic eating and sleeping habits because they are chief constituents of our physical dimension. As they say, 'We become what we eat'.

While explaining the concept of yoga to Arjuna, lord Krishna also throws light on this:

yuktāhāra-vihārasya
yukta-ceṣṭasyakarmasu
yukta-svapnāvabodhasya
yogobhavatiduḥkha-hā

"He who is regulated in his habits of eating, sleeping, recreation and work can mitigate all material pains by practicing the yoga system."
– *Bhagavad Gita 6.17*

Exercise is also an important element of our physical dimension and it needs to be inculcated in our daily schedule. Spending 30 minutes for exercise is worth it, considering the tremendous benefits that it is going to have in terms of the impact, on the other 1440 minutes of the day.

Those who say they don't have enough time to exercise, for them I would love to quote Edward Stanley who once said, "Those who think they have no time for bodily exercise will sooner or later have to find time for illness."

A well taken care of physical dimension will include – a healthy body, a strong body, a flexible body, a body in proper shape, a body efficient at work, a body with competent senses and a body that can endure.

The Mental dimension:

Mind is a very subtle but powerful dimension. If our body is compared to hardware, then the mind can be compared to software. If the software is corrupted, then no matter how good your physical device is, it can't function effectively.

The mind is also a storehouse of all our emotions and it enables us to think, feel and function. By nature, the mind is flickering and hence it is said, "Mind can create hell out of heaven and heaven out of hell."

If your mind is not under control, it can weaken your determination, cause stress, depression and hypertension. It can also cause other negative influences. A wayward mind is like an uncontrolled wick of a lamp which can only give soot and darkness but, if properly controlled, can give light. If the mind is tamed, it can help you attain your desired goal. The same message is seen in the pages of *Bhagavad Gita*,

> *Bandhurātmātmanastasya*
> *yenātmaivātmanājitaḥ*
> *anātmanastuśatrutve*
> *vartetātmaivaśatru-vat*

"For him who has conquered the mind, the mind is the best of friends; but for one who has failed to do so, his mind will remain the greatest enemy."

– *Bhagavad Gita* 6.6

Our ability to function is directly proportional to the stability of our mind. Hence we must spend some time for the development of our mental dimension. I am sharing few tips which you can implement to achieve the same:

a. Reading- There's no better way to enrich and expand your mind than to get into the habit of reading good books.

   Mark Twain puts it succinctly, "The man who does not read good books has no advantage over the man who can't read them." Dr Josie Billington, deputy director of the Centre for Research into Reading at the University of Liverpool says, "Reading can offer richer, broader, and more complex models of experience, which enable people to view their own lives from a refreshed perspective and with renewed understanding."

Spending some time on reading on a daily basis is always better than mindlessly watching TV and surfing on the internet.

b. Writing– Writing is yet another powerful tool to develop the mental dimension. Keeping a journal of thoughts, experiences, and learnings improves our ability to think clearly and reason accurately.

c. Meditation– Meditation is for the mind, what food is to the body. It helps in an all-inclusive way, re-energizing you and thereby helping you to control your mind. Recent research has shown that meditation is good for the brain. It improves the immune system, reduces stress and promotes a sense of well-being.

d. Yogasanas and breathing exercises– Yoga, combined with proper deep and rhythmic breathing, is an easy and healthy way of uplifting the mind. Yogasanas are not just physical exercises, but rather very subtle processes to manipulate one's energy in a particular direction.

A well taken care of mental dimension will include – a mind that is stable and clear, a mind that is focused and peaceful, a mind that is satisfied and a mind which has the ability to think critically and deal sensitively.

The Social dimension:

Human beings are social animals and life, by nature, is interdependent. This dimension refers to our ability to maintain meaningful relationships with other members of not only our family, but also our larger society. Nurturing relationships enrich our life and make it fulfilling. Developing this dimension does not take so much of time compared to the other dimensions. We can do it in our regular everyday interactions with other people. But it definitely requires some exercise.

The pace of life today is such that often, relationships are given a low priority in our list of things that we need to take care of. It is important that our relationships are built on firm ground, since they become a strong social support for us. They play an important role in helping us to lead a healthy and stress-free life.

The obvious question that comes to mind is –
how do I improve this dimension of life? Here are
few tips:

a. Developing a good character– Character in life is
   what makes people believe in you. It is essential
   for both individual success and for our society to
   function harmoniously. Every individual must do
   their part by living a life of integrity. The reality
   is that quality relationships are built on principles
   especially trust.

b. Dealing sensitively– Everyone around us is a
   sentient being, having emotions. If we do not
   deal with others sensitively, we could ruin our
   relationships with them. The golden rule to deal
   with others can be found in almost all religions
   and cultures. Here is a reference from the great
   epic *Mahabharata*,

   Tasmāddharma-pradhānéna
   bhavitavyamyatātmanā |
   tathā cha sarva-bhūtéṣhu
   vartitavyamyathātmani ||
   [Mahābhārata, Shānti-Parva 167:9]

   "Thus, by self-control and by making dharma
   (right conduct) your main focus, treat others as
   you treat yourself."

Ask yourself a question. 'Does my tone of voice, body language and behaviour reflect sensitivity while dealing with others?'

c. Being a good listener– The most basic of all human needs is the need to understand and be understood.

The best way to understand people is to listen to them. Listening is the first thing we do when we come into this world. We spend years learning how to read, write and speak, but what about listening? Listening is used the most, but taught the least. We have to learn the art of empathic listening which allows us to develop and enhance relationships with a stronger understanding of what is being conveyed, both intellectually and emotionally.

Glynn David Harris of International Listening Association puts is aptly, "When you've learned how to listen, well that's when you've learned everything you need to know in your life!"

d. Selfless service– We can't talk of love without talking about selfless service. This type of service can win hearts of people. There is an intrinsic security that comes from authentic and genuine service, from helping people in a meaningful way. Muhammad Ali once rightly said, "Service to others is the rent you pay for the room here on earth."

So be creative to find ways and means to serve others. A well taken care of social dimension will include-being friendly, being a good listener, being sensitive to others, needs and concerns, being trustworthy, being cooperative, being forgiving and loving.

The Spiritual dimension:

Spiritual dimension is our changeless core, which is a part of the Supreme Lord, source of all life in this world. The spiritual dimension involves exploring the key principles, beliefs and values that give meaning and purpose to your life. It's about living in a way that is consistent with timeless principles.

When we live superficial lives, dedicated to serving ourselves, we are like surfers; riding the waves, but not seeing what is beneath them. We may satisfy our own needs and concerns by doing so, but we will never be truly fulfilled. However, when we practice spirituality, we become like divers; we submerge ourselves underneath the turbulent waves to find a pleasure which is much deeper and beyond hedonistic ideals. That profound joy is only possible when one loves to serve others. And one feels that love through being connected to god through spirituality.

Jesus Christ said in the *Bible*, "The highest commandment is to love thy God with all thy soul and all thy might and thy heart." He then said that because of following the highest commandment of loving god we begin to "love thy neighbour as thy self." This means when we become spiritual minded and experience the love of god, we feel compassion for the pain of others.

Buddha once said, 'Just as a candle cannot burn without fire, we cannot live without spiritual life.'

How do we improve our spiritual dimension? Here are few tips:

a. Reading scriptures – Scriptures are called word of god and contain those universal principles which guide human beings and they offer us a destination worth going to. Every religion has their set of scriptures. Reading scriptures is one of the ways to develop our connection with god. It helps us to rise on our maturity continuum. A genuine spiritual aspirant not only reads scriptures passively, but also tries to actively live by them.

b. Associating with saintly people – Saintly people are those great souls who experience the love of god and share the same with the entire humanity. Just by being close to a flower, we get the fragrance; similarly associating with saintly people is the easiest way to experience the same love they possess.

c. Chanting prayers – Prayers are the powerful and easiest way to communicate with god at any time. Today, major religions involve praying in one way or another. These can be prayers of gratitude, prayers to create a positive change in our lives, prayers to ask for the strength to deal with a variety of situations, prayers for well-being of every living entity and so on.

d. Loving service – When you get big good news, you want to share it with others. Similarly, a heart which loves god wants to share it with others. A person who loves god or wants to love god can't see the suffering of others. He always wants to alleviate their suffering and is ready to go to any extent for that. He is always eager to help people and uplift their consciousness.

A well taken care of spiritual dimension will include a sense of meaning and purpose in life, being well connected with god through prayers, meditation and reading scriptures, sharing the love of god to people in general and, being grateful and blissful.

All the four dimensions of life can be compared to four rooms of a house where we live – physical, mental, social and a spiritual room. Most of us tend to live in one room most of the time, but unless we go into every room every day, even if to keep it aired, we are not complete.

Remember, success in one area can't compensate for failure in other areas of life.

Q 7.   Some people say that you should have a daily timetable, some people say, you should have a weekly timetable. Which is better and what is the best practice to make it?

Ans.   It's a good practice to make a timetable for your activities. It gives a structure to your day and you don't miss on important things. It's a tool that will assist you so that you don't lose your energy later in managing crises. Let me share my own experience.

Hearing a spiritual masters' discourse is of paramount importance for a monk. We call it *Vani Seva*, which means listening to spiritual master and serving him by following his instructions.

I used to listen to recorded discourses of my spiritual master, but not so frequently. Once, after hearing its importance from one senior monk in the ashram, I decided that I will listen to the discourse of my spiritual master daily. Hence, I included it in my daily timetable. Then, I was able to listen to discourses daily but faced a lot of problems on Saturday and Sunday because I was counselling students and few families. They would meet me in temple on weekends because colleges and other institutions have weekly off on either Saturday or Sunday.

Not being able to commit to my new discipline of hearing a spiritual masters' discourse daily was putting me into the pool of guilt. I even started considering weekends as burdensome as I was feeling undisciplined.

So I approached my mentor, another senior monk in our ashram and told him my entire problem.

"See, Krishna Dhan," he said calmly, "When you counsel people on weekends, you are helping them to come out of their problems. You may not be able to listen to your spiritual masters' discourses on those days but you are adhering to his instructions through counselling others.

"Do not try to fit everything in a single day. Why don't you make a weekly schedule instead? Organising on a weekly basis provides much greater balance than daily planning. Your self-organisational tool should deal not only with schedules but also with people. There will be times when you will have to prioritise people over schedule. Your tool needs to reflect that value, to facilitate implementation rather than create guilt when a schedule is not followed. Your planning tool should be flexible. It should be your servant, never your master."

"What you are saying makes perfect sense to me, but I think I have too many roles to play. Do you mean I should cut down some of them?" I questioned.

"Sit calmly and write down all the roles which you play in your life, the areas where you wish to invest your time and energy on a regular basis. You may have to play the role of an individual, brother, son, disciple of a spiritual master, mentor, temple administrator and so on," replied my mentor.

Sensing a perplexed look on my face, he immediately said, "Don't get bothered about roles that define you for the rest of your life. Just consider a week and write down the areas on which you see yourself spending time on during the next seven days. Now think of some important results you wish to accomplish in each role during the next seven days."

"What do you mean by 'result in each role'?" I interrupted.

"These are goals pertaining to roles. For instance, as a mentor, you might have to meet few students in a week and counsel them. As a disciple of a spiritual master, you might have to listen to few of his discourses. As an administrator of the temple, see if any administrative work is pending and so on," he replied immediately.

"Seems great! What next?" I asked.

He then replied, "Now you can look at the week ahead with your goals in mind and schedule time to achieve them. There are some goals that you may only be able to accomplish during week days and, some only on Sunday when colleges and businesses have a weekly off.

"Saturday and Sunday are busy for me too. Hence, I have decided to do yoga only five days a week and that's perfectly fine. Having identified your roles and associated goals, you can translate each goal to a specific day of a week. You can also check your annual or monthly calendar for any appointments you may have previously made and adjust your schedule accordingly.

"With weekly organizing, daily planning becomes merely a function of adapting and prioritising activities. Take out few minutes each morning to review your schedule. It would put you in touch with the value-based decision you made as you organized the week. As you look at the overview of your day, you will experience a sense of balance as the roles and associated goals provide natural prioritisation."

"Wow! Simply amazing!" These were the only words that came from my mouth. I thanked him and returned with a new vision of living a balanced life on weekly basis.

You won't believe, from that day, I followed exactly what he suggested and my time-management reached to the next level. Weekly organizing gave me the freedom and flexibility to handle unanticipated events. I could easily shift appointments whenever needed. I started viewing 168 hours a week, rather than just 24 hours a day. And most importantly, I was now savouring my interactions with people on weekends which were burdensome before meeting my mentor.

And if you ask me now, I listen to my spiritual masters' discourses five days a week in the afternoon. I do yoga five days a week in the morning. I run a programme for teenagers 'Samruddhi School of Leadership' every Sunday. I meet a group of families and interact with them every Tuesday evening. I worship deities in the temple twice a week. I am a weekly man now.

To conclude, having experienced the power of principle-centered weekly organization in my own life, I can say with confidence that it works. It has transformed the lives of hundreds of people. This approach can really make a lot of positive difference when we talk about balanced living.

Author's Note

In this book, we have discussed a set of 6 Ss of self-improvement. But, why 5.5 Ss and not 6 Ss? Let me explain.

We have discussed the story of Milo of Croton in chapter 4. Therein we discussed how:

He selected his area of improvement (first S) – Body building.

He started with small weight (second S) – He began with a new-born calf.

He had a schedule for performing the task (third S) – He would do it every day.

He took advantage of his surroundings (fourth S) – Tiny increase in weight of the calf which was near his household.

He stayed on (fifth S) – He did this for almost 3-4 years.

Our last 'S' is 'Seek Help' (either through accountability or feed forward method). But somehow, I did not notice this last 'S' in case of Milo. Because I have developed these 5 Ss based on the story of Milo, and the sixth 'S' has no connection to that story, I have rated the last 'S' as half.

Over the decades, many organisations have increased their level of performance and got benefited by the 5 'S' – one of the tools of Kaizen.

You can make use of the 5.5 'S' mentioned in this book to take your life to the next level. These techniques have helped me as well as those innumerable people who have sought guidance from me in last two decades. And these techniques are there for you as well, if you wish to change for better.

Remember no institution, book, therapist, or workshop will help a person improve unless he or she really has the willingness to change.

Before launching our life to a higher level, let us see three different levels of people from a Sanskrit verse by great poet Bhartrhari:

prarabhyate na khalu vighnabhayena nichaih
prarabhya vighnavihata viramanti madhyah ||
vighnaih punah punarapi pratihanyamanah
prarabdhamuttamaguaa na parityajanti ||

There are three types of people – lower, middle and higher. Lower grade people are those who do not start their work upon seeing imminent difficulties. Middle grade people start the work but when difficulties come, they give up the work without completing it. But higher grade people are those who, in spite of so many difficulties on their path, do not give up on the work which they have undertaken without completing it.

So, whatever level you are situated at, now is the right time to go to a higher level. Then, keep moving upward and launch your life to the highest level. You can dramatically enhance the overall quality of your life, provided you opt for improvement. All you need is the desire to become better, the decision to act, the discipline to practice, and the determination to persist until you get the desired result.

Thomas Jefferson has expressed a very thought-provoking idea. "If you want something you've never had, you must be willing to do something you've never done."

All the best for your improvement journey'!

I hope this book will act as a beacon light on your journey. 'Seek help' of this book whenever you stumble on your improvement journey. I personally struggle with much of what I have shared in this book. But the struggle is worthwhile and fulfilling. We do not have to worry; the almighty is there to help us out.

As it is rightly said, 'god helps those, who help themselves.

List of Acronyms

References

A.C. Bhaktivedanta Swami Prabhupada – *Bhagavad Gita – As it is.* The Bhaktivedanta Book Trust, 1986

Clear, James. *Atomic Habits: Tiny changes, remarkable results.* Random House Business Books, 2018

Duckworth, Angela. *Grit – The Power of Passion and Perseverance.* Scribner, 2016

Dweck, Carol. *Mindset: Changing the Way You Think to Fulfil Your Potential.* Constable & Robinson, 2012

Gawande, Atul. *The Checklist Manifesto: How to get things right.* Penguin Books India, 2014

Guise, Stephen. *Mini Habits: Smaller Habits, Bigger Results.* Lightning Source Inc, 2013

Goldsmith Marshall & Reiter Mark – *What got you here won't get you there.* Hachette India

Hardy Darren – *The Compound Effect – Jumpstart your income, your life, your success.* Da Capo, 2013

Imai, Masaaki. *Kaizen: The Key to Japan's Competitive Success.* McGraw-Hill Education, 1988

Koch, Richard. *The 80/20 Principle: The secret to achieving more with less*. RHUS, 1999

Maurer, Dr Robert . *One Small Step Can Change Your Life: The Kaizen Way*. Algonquin Books, 2014

Rubin, Gretchen. *Better than before – Mastering the habits of our everyday lives*. Two Roads: 2017

Sean Covey & Chris McChesney: *The 4 Disciplines of Execution: Achieving Your Wildly Important Goals, Simon & Schuster*, 2012

Stephen R. Covey: 7 *Habits of Highly Effective People- Powerful lessons in personal change, Simon & Schuster*, 2004